De Stijl was the name of the magazine founded in 1917 by the Dutch painter, designer and writer, Theo van Doesburg and edited by him until his death in 1931. De Stijl is Dutch for The Style and many of those who contributed to the magazine or who were associated with De Stijl showed its characteristic style in their work—rectangularity and the use of pure colour, the absence of decoration, a belief in abstraction and a humanism that rejected the natural for the man-made. Amongst those associated with De Stijl were the architects Rietveld, Oud, van t'Hoff and van Eesteren, the painters Mondrian, van der Leck and Huszar, and the sculptor Vantongerloo.

Previous accounts have tended to overstress the importance of painting in De Stijl (and of the work of Mondrian in particular). Without doubting that Mondrian is one of the few really great modern painters, Paul Overy attempts to redress the balance by emphasizing the contribution of the architects and designers and van Doesburg himself.

De Stijl was one of the formative factors in the developments of the 'twenties and 'thirties in architecture, product and graphic design and in painting and sculpture. Its impact is still felt today.

In this account, De Stijl is not treated as an isolated phenomenon but related to the international and Dutch background, to Art Nouveau, Cubism, Futurism, Constructivism and the Bauhaus.

Paul Overy was born in 1940. He has taught in schools and art colleges and written regular art criticism and reviews for *The Listener*, *The Financial Times* and *Art and Artists*. He has contributed articles and reviews to various other magazines and has worked in television. He has recently published a critical study of Kandinsky.

Van Doesburg (right) and **Van Eesteren** working on models for
the De Stijl exhibition in Paris, 1923

Paul Overy

DE STIJL

studio vista|dutton pictureback
General editor David Herbert

© Paul Overy 1969
Designed by Gillian Greenwood
Published in Great Britain by Studio Vista Limited
Blue Star House, Highgate Hill, London N 19
and in the USA by E. P. Dutton and Co. Inc.
201 Park Avenue South, New York, NY 10003
Set in 8D Univers on 11 pt
Made and printed in Great Britain by
Richard Clay (The Chaucer Press), Ltd.
Bungay, Suffolk

SBN: 289 79622 9 (cased)
     289 79621 0 (paperback)

Contents

Introduction

Gerrit Rietveld's red-blue armchair is the most compact visual statement of the principles of De Stijl. Visually separate and discrete, each square-sectioned wooden member which makes up the structural frame of the chair extends beyond its point of juncture, probing the space that surrounds the chair as well as defining the space that flows freely through it.

There is no dovetailing. Where the wooden rails cross they are held together by wooden pins. The plywood planks of seat and back are fixed to this frame. The chair discloses its structure as clearly as a skeleton or scaffolding. The seat is painted blue, the back red. The frame is black with the sawn ends of each rail painted yellow. Rietveld wrote about this chair: 'The construction is attuned to the parts to insure that no part dominates or is subordinate to the others. In this way, the whole stands freely and clearly in space, and the form stands out from the material.'

De Stijl is Dutch for The Style. Not style as implied in 'styling' (car styling, etc)—a package wrapped round the working parts, the icing on the cake—but Style as the integral relationship of the parts to the whole and of the whole to the parts. 'Unity in Plurality' was the definition of Style given by the Dutch architect H.P.Berlage whose buildings and writings were important influences in the early development of De Stijl.

Gerrit Rietveld Red-blue armchair, 1917 or 1918
Collection Stedelijk Museum, Amsterdam

Theo van Doesburg *Counter-composition* 1925
Oil. Van Doesburg's diagonals were more dynamic and disturbing than those
of Rietveld and van der Leck. Collection Haags Gemeentemuseum, The Hague

8

Vilmos Huszar *Composition De Stijl* 1916
Oil. The painting on which the cover of *De Stijl* was based until 1921. Loan
Dienst voor's Rijks Verspride Kuntsvoorwerpen. Collection Haags
Gemeentemuseum, The Hague

De Stijl was not a group in the usual sense. It takes its name from
the magazine edited by the Dutch painter, designer and writer,
Theo van Doesburg from 1917 to 1931. Many of those associated
with De Stijl met only briefly and some of the most important
like Rietveld and Mondrian never met at all. Many disassociated
themselves from De Stijl fairly early in their careers, like

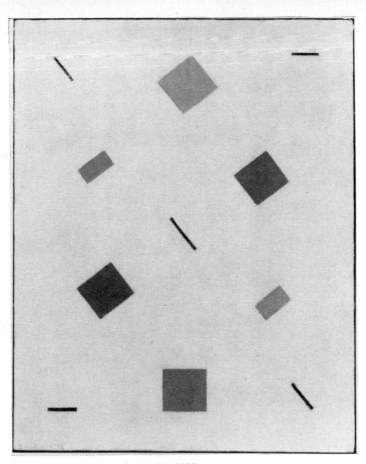

Bart van der Leck *Composition* 1918
Oil. Diagonals appeared early in De Stijl painting (as in Rietveld's chair).
Collection Tate Gallery, London

Bart van der Leck and J.P.Oud, but their work did not change fundamentally as a result of this. Sometimes their most typical De Stijl work was produced after they had left. That they continued to respect van Doesburg even when they had disagreed or fallen out with him, or he with them, is clear from their tributes to him in the final, memorial issue of the *De Stijl* magazine.

Georges Vantongerloo *Construction S* $\times \frac{R}{3}$ 1933
Iron. The planes fly out like the black rails of Rietveld's chair. Courtesy
Marlborough Gallery, London

In the later development of De Stijl, van Doesburg 'recruited'
some artists whose work had little in common with the earlier
phase of De Stijl, and in retrospect he tended to exaggerate the
extent to which there had been a coherent group. In a sense, only
van Doesburg himself and the magazine he edited were 'De Stijl'.
When he died in 1931 the magazine ceased publication shortly
afterwards and De Stijl as a compelling idea died with him, but its
spirit remained in the work of many of those who had been associated with it or who had been inspired or influenced by its ideals.
The style remained.

Piet Mondrian *Composition with Red, Yellow and Blue* 1936–42
The three-dimensional complexity of Rietveld's chair is achieved in two
dimensions. Collection Tate Gallery, London

In another sense De Stijl was only the work of those artists and architects whose work embodied the principles of De Stijl, who had its style. But these principles were not static ; it was a style that evolved. Although Mondrian left De Stijl when van Doesburg introduced the diagonal element and justified it in theoretical statements, this was not a betrayal of the earlier principles of horizontal–vertical, but an intelligent development of it which is already foreshadowed in 1918 in Rietveld's red-blue chair or van der Leck's paintings.

In the first issue of the *De Stijl* magazine in 1917 van Doesburg had written : 'For the propagation of the beautiful, a spiritual group is more necessary than a social one.' Despite the emphasis on the universal and the abstract in statements and essays, De Stijl remained a loose association of individualists.

When Rietveld designed his red-blue chair he was not yet associated with De Stijl. When J.P.Oud designed the Café Unie in Rotterdam, a marvellous combination of line, colour and lettering, he had already severed his connection. Yet both designs are unmistakably De Stijl. Clearly what unites them is Style, not physical or ideological adherence to a movement or group.

1 The international background

Styles in art and architecture do not develop in a vacuum. Certain elements in De Stijl can undoubtedly be related to the Dutch background, but there are important parallels and precursors in art and architecture elsewhere in Europe, and in America.

The pre-eminence of England in architecture and the applied arts towards the end of the nineteenth century was short-lived but influential on the Continent. The writings of William Morris and other

E.W.Godwin Sideboard, 1867
Collection Victoria and Albert Museum. Crown Copyright

designers were widely read in Europe and the work of English designers was well known both from periodicals and from exhibitions.

The exterior of the white house which Edward Godwin designed for Whistler in 1878 was plain and unassuming—white-painted brick with windows and doors placed asymmetrically. Godwin's interiors and furniture, which show his early interest in Japanese design, were even more striking in their simplicity and clearness of construction. Godwin's buffet and a chair, both of which are now in the Victoria and Albert Museum in London, seem to anticipate Rietveld's red-blue chair and buffet (see page 26).

E. W. Godwin Chair, about 1885
Collection Victoria and Albert Museum, Crown Copyright

In England the influence of Morris meant that the well-designed furniture produced at the end of the nineteenth century and the beginning of the twentieth century was produced by hand and hence could only be afforded by a rich and cultured élite. In Germany, however, designers were beginning to design for the machine, with the result that good design became more generally available.

Between 1896 and 1903 Hermann Muthesius was posted in England as a supplementary trade attaché at the German Embassy to study English architecture and design and to report on its development—a kind of cultural spy. He published the results of his stay in three volumes entitled *Das Englische Haus* (The English House) which covered every aspect of English domestic architecture. From Muthesius' books and articles the De Stijl architects, like most of their continental contemporaries, would have been familiar with developments in English design.

In 1907, under Muthesius' leadership, some of the more enterprising German manufacturers together with architects and designers formed the Deutscher Werkbund to improve standards of quality in industrial design.

In 1905–6 Richard Riemerschmid had designed his first machine-made furniture for the Deutsche Werkstätten, and in 1907 the Werkstätten commissioned designs for mass-produced low-cost furniture from Bruno Paul and this was exhibited in 1910 as the first unit furniture (*Typemöbel*).

In Germany and Austria the firm of Thonet had been producing bentwood furniture in their factories by mass-production techniques since the middle of the nineteenth century. The beechwood parts were steamed and bent mechanically in large numbers and later assembled to make up the individual chairs. The famous café chair, No. 14, was first made in 1859 and by 1910 had sold over fifty million. The design is still in use today and what is more is still made and sold.

Although curvilinear in form rather than angular, Thonet's chairs anticipate Rietveld's furniture in that the pieces are fixed together so that they remain visually separate and stand out clearly in space. Although Rietveld's furniture was never mass-produced it was designed in such a way that this would be possible. The red-blue armchair, for instance, is based on a module, and the parts are standardized and absolutely simple. Rietveld's designs are rather

Thonet Desk chair no. 9, designed 1855

like early prototypes for mass-produced furniture. They have been regarded as such by later designers who have plundered them for ideas.

In the early years of the twentieth century the Scottish architect, Charles Rennie Mackintosh, was well known on the Continent although hardly at all in England. Reproductions of his executed works and projected designs were published in European art and

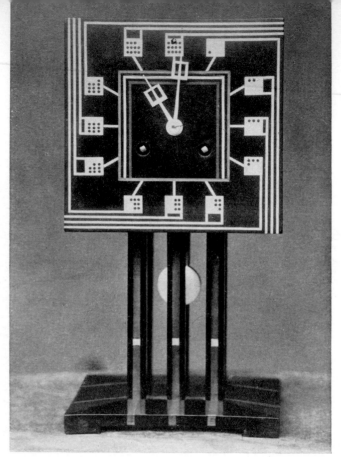

Charles Rennie Mackintosh Clock, *c.* 1917–19
Ebonized wood with ivory inlay. Collection University of Glasgow

design journals. Recently attempts have been made to locate
Mackintosh in the tradition of nineteenth-century architecture and
design rather than as a pioneer of the Modern Movement, but un-
deniably he was a precursor of much twentieth-century architecture and interior design if not necessarily an active influence. By
the time of the First World War he had fallen into obscurity, although one of his most interesting designs, the conversion of a
house in Northampton, was done in 1916–17.

In 1908 the Austrian architect Adolf Loos, Hoffmann's exact
contemporary, wrote an essay entitled *Ornament and Crime* in
which decoration was equated with primitivism or decadence: 'I

Charles Rennie Mackintosh main staircase Glasgow School of Art, 1896–9

have evolved the following maxim, and pronounce it to the world: the evolution of culture marches with the elimination of ornament from useful objects.' (The arrogance and dogmatism of this could only have come out of the Vienna of Freud and Krafft-Ebing.) In his Steiner house, Loos puts his theories into practice, no ornament disfigures its plain surfaces and blank windows.

In the Carson, Pirie and Scott department store (Chicago), designed by Louis Sullivan, the façade is built from horizontal bands of windows. In earlier buildings like the Wainwright building in St Louis and the Guaranty building in Buffalo, Sullivan had stressed the vertical structural elements. Here the emphasis is transferred to the horizontal, and to the window area rather than the structural elements. The window bands are carried right round the corner of the building—a solution that was later to be used frequently by European architects like Erich Mendelsohn in the design of

Opposite
Louis Sullivan Carson, Pirie and Scott department store,
Chicago, Illinois, 1899–1904

Walter Gropius and **Adolf Meyer** Fagus shoe-last factory,
Alfeld-an-der-Leine, 1911

Frank Lloyd Wright Unity Temple, Chicago, 1906

department stores and other commercial buildings. Oud used similar means in the rounded ends of terraces in his two estates at Hook of Holland and Kiefhoek (pages 137 and 143). The horizontal 'Chicago windows' had been used earlier by architects like Burnham and Root, but Sullivan's combination of these with the rounded corner, preserving the unity of a single façade as it curves through the right angle of the street corner, represents a dramatic and revolutionary step into the twentieth century.

The Chicago window with its combination of larger and smaller panes of glass is slightly reminiscent of some of Mondrian and van Doesburg's paintings of 1921 (see page 29). The influence of the painting of Mondrian and van Doesburg on the architecture of the early nineteen-twenties has often been claimed. However, if there *was* an influence from their work it was clearly more a matter of

Frank Lloyd Wright Robie house, Chicago, 1909

clarifying elements which were already present in the work of architects like Sullivan.

The early buildings of Sullivan's pupil, Frank Lloyd Wright, were the most important non-Dutch influences on the architects who were first associated with De Stijl, Robert van t'Hoff, Jan Wils and Oud. Wright's work and ideas were introduced to Holland through an exhibition in 1910 and the two Wasmuth volumes (in German) on Wright in 1910 and 1911. Berlage saw Wright's buildings when he visited America in 1911 and lectured on Sullivan, Richardson and particularly Wright on his return. A little later van t'Hoff went to Chicago and met Wright. He came back to Holland in 1914 full of enthusiasm for his work and his two villas at Huis ter Heide near Utrecht were inspired by Wright's work. Wright's Robie house, with its great horizontal emphasis and dramatically cantilevered

25

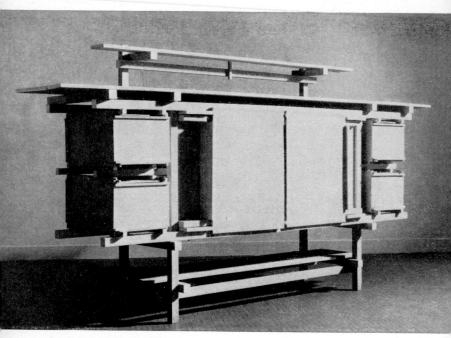

Gerrit Rietveld Buffet, 1919
Collection Mr & Mrs Brian Housden

eaves, offers very clear visual parallels with the most advanced three-dimensional works associated with De Stijl, like Rietveld's buffet, red-blue chair and Schröder house and Vantongerloo's later sculpture. Rietveld was asked to make Wrightian furniture for van t'Hoff's larger villa in 1918, but this was quite possibly after he had

Robert van t' Hoff Villa at Huis ter Heide, near Utrecht, 1916

already made the buffet and the red-blue chair. Rietveld may well have arrived at his solutions independently as a result of the careful analysis of the process of making a piece of furniture, stripping it down to the bare essentials, exposing the skeletal structure of small pieces of wood that underlies even a conventional chair.

Musical instruments' room, Imperial Katsura Palace, Kyoto, seventeenth century

There is a strong Japanese quality to Rietveld's early furniture (particularly the buffet). The balanced asymmetry and contemplative silence of Mondrian's later paintings are in extraordinary sympathy with Japanese interiors. Van Doesburg had written articles on Japanese and Asiatic art in the magazine *Eenheid*, 1912–13.

When Mondrian moved to Paris in 1911 he quickly found that Cubism offered a solution to the problems he had been struggling with in Holland. It enabled him first to clarify the function of line and then later, more slowly, that of the plane in his work. Possibly

Piet Mondrian *Composition with Red, Yellow and Blue* 1921
Oil. Loan S.B. Slijper, Collection Haags Gemeentemuseum,
The Hague

he might have arrived at these without the help of Cubism, but it would certainly have taken longer.

Very soon Mondrian had gone far beyond the static, intellectual unpicking of the seams of reality of Cubism. In an autobiographical essay written shortly before his death Mondrian recalled: 'Gradually I became aware that Cubism did not accept the logical consequences of its own discoveries; it was not developing abstraction towards the ultimate goal, the expression of pure reality.' Between 1912 and his return to Holland in 1914 his work is a gradual and very sensitive rendering down of visual reality to the plane surface and the rectilinear juncture of horizontal and vertical lines.

Oud frequently referred to the influence of Cubism on his own work, on the other De Stijl architects, and on the Modern Movement in architecture in general. But there is very little evidence of the influence of painting in modern architecture at all. All the elements are there in the Chicago School, in Wright, in Loos.

Drawings for projected buildings by the Futurist architects Antonio Sant'Elia and Mario Chiattone were published in the *De Stijl* magazine with commentaries by van t'Hoff and Oud, and the futurist painter Gino Severini contributed several articles.

Unlike the Cubists, the Futurists were interested in finding forms to express the newness of twentieth-century experience. Some of their techniques were borrowed from Cubism, but it was techniques only. The angular lines of force in Futurist painting and sculpture were derived from multiple exposure photography like the 'chronophotographs' of E.-J. Marey. The influence of this is most obvious in Balla's comic painting of a scampering dachshund with its legs and tail depicted as fans of whirling lines. Later these elements were assimilated into more abstract forms.

The dynamic diagonals of van Doesburg's counter-compositions seem related to these lines of force in Futurism; a dramatic abstract expression of movement. It is perhaps not too far-fetched to see a parallel also in the angled planes of Rietveld's red-blue chair, although like other early works of De Stijl this is static and balanced, not dynamic.

Piet Mondrian *Composition in Oval* 1913/14
Oil. Loan S.N. Slijper. Collection Haags Gemeentemuseum, The Hague

The excessively romantic, almost demonic worship of speed and machinery of the Futurists becomes a sober and seemingly rational analysis in the writings of van Doesburg, Mondrian and Oud.

We will sing of the nocturnal vibration of arsenals and workshops beneath their violent electric moons . . . of adventurous steamers scenting the horizon; of broad-chested locomotives prancing on the rails, like huge steel horses bridled with long tubes; and of the gliding flight of aeroplanes, the sound of their propellers like the flapping of flags and the applause of an enthusiastic crowd. (Marinetti: Futurist Manifesto)

The machine is, *par excellence*, a phenomenon of spiritual discipline. Materialism as a way of life and art took handicraft as its direct psychological expression. The new spiritual artistic sensibility of the twentieth century has not only felt the beauty of the machine, but has also taken cognisance of its unlimited expressive possibilities for the arts. (Van Doesburg)

Mondrian was a member of the Dutch Theosophical Society and kept a picture of Madame Blavatsky in his studio. It is customary today to think of theosophy as middle-brow, half-baked and rather laughable. This is arrogant prejudice. A way of thinking which attracted men as intelligent as Mondrian, Yeats, Kandinsky, Scriabin and Stravinsky must have had something important to offer, particularly in the context of the opposition to late nineteenth, early twentieth-century scientific positivism and materialism. From theosophy possibly comes the similarity of some De Stijl ideas (the universal as opposed to the individual) to Buddhism and other Eastern religious teaching. Rietveld was interested in the writings of the Bengali poet, Rabrindranath Tagore.

Antonio Sant' Elia Design for a building, 1914.
This drawing by Sant' Elia was reproduced in *De Stijl*, 1919 (Vol 11 No 10)

In the last paragraph of his theoretical essay *Concerning the Spiritual in Art* (published 1912) Kandinsky wrote:

We are fast approaching a time of reasoned and conscious composition, in which the painter will be proud to declare his work constructional—this in contrast to the claim of the Impressionists that they could explain nothing, that their art came by inspiration We have before us an age of conscious creation, and this new spirit in painting is going hand in hand with thought towards an *epoch of great spirituality*.

Van Doesburg read Kandinsky's book shortly after it appeared and championed his work and ideas in the reviews and essays that he contributed to various Dutch periodicals. There are several of van Doesburg's early paintings which show the influence of the expressionist abstract paintings that Kandinsky was producing in Munich up to 1914. Kandinsky's work of this period was, on the surface at least, rather different from the 'reasoned and conscious composition' that he looked forward to in his book. His own work did not finally become geometrical until the early 'twenties. Sooner than Kandinsky himself, van Doesburg came to reject the intuitive, expressionist method of composition, but his belief in 'the spiritual in art' remained constant to the end of his life.

Kasimir Malevitch *Suprematist Composition* 1915
Oil. Malevitch's suprematist works were possibly an influence on van Doesburg's diagonal counter-compositions. Collection Stedelijk Museum, Amsterdam.

35

2 The Dutch background

In Holland one is always aware of the line of the horizon. Against it a tree, a man, a building stands out as a vertical which makes an angle of ninety degrees with the horizon—the horizontal.

The Dutch landscape is not natural. It is almost entirely man-made, reclaimed from the sea and dependant on a complex system of rectangular dykes and polders. Holland is the most densely populated country in the world (900 people to the square mile).

Many of the larger towns, particularly in the western part of Holland between Amsterdam, the Hague, Rotterdam and Utrecht are only a few minutes apart by train or car. In no other country is there less discontinuity between the countryside and the town. The Dutch countryside is as *un*-natural, as man-made as the town. In Holland they say 'God made the World, the Dutch made Holland'.

The straight line and the right angle are, with the plane surface, the most important elements in De Stijl. (Van Doesburg originally thought of calling the magazine '*The Straight Line*'.) They seem to stand for man's control of his environment. Nowhere is this ordering and discipline of nature more apparent than in Holland. It is, in fact, the great achievement of the Dutch people who have reclaimed so much of their country from the sea and made habitable what was previously uninhabitable.

However, as H.L.C.Jaffé (the author of the standard work on De Stijl) has stressed, it is necessary to avoid the suggestion that in adopting the straight line and the plane surface the De Stijl artists were indulging in a 'camouflaged naturalism': 'The Dutch landscape has been built *according to the same principles* upon which the work of De Stijl is founded'—the one does not depend upon the other.

It would be a mistake to over-emphasize the importance of national and local factors in the development of De Stijl. No doubt the flatness and un-naturalness of the Dutch landscape contributed to the emphasis on the horizontal and vertical and the plane surface in the work of De Stijl, but the tendency towards rectilinearity and geometric form was common to all the countries which contributed to the modern movement in art and architecture during the first decades of the century.

In the past in Dutch town architecture it has been the vertical which has most often been stressed. In De Stijl architecture the horizontal and vertical are balanced, or if one element predominates it is the horizontal—but again this is common to the international development of architecture at this time.

Some of the ideas inherent in De Stijl may derive from the Dutch Jewish philosopher Spinoza (1632–77) ; Spinoza believed that individual souls and separate objects were not things, but aspects of the Divine Being (God). He rejected the personal immortality of Christianity. The only immortality possible was in becoming more and more one with God.

Spinoza wrote 'all determination is negation'—things are defined by their boundaries, that is, where they change into something else. (There is a constant insistence in the writings of the De Stijl artists on *relations* rather than things.)

Spinoza's *Ethics* is laid out like Euclid's Geometry with definitions, axioms and theorems. The last two books are entitled : *Of Human Bondage, or The Strength of the Emotions* and *Of the Power of the Understanding, or of Human Freedom.*

Van Doesburg wrote : 'Every emotion, be it grief or joy, implies a rupture of harmony, of equilibrium between the subject (man) and the object (universe).'

According to Spinoza passions distract us and obscure our intellectual vision of the whole. . . . 'Spiritual unhealthiness and misfortunes can generally be traced to excessive love of something which is subject to many variations.' On the other hand spiritual health lies in 'love towards a thing immutable and eternal'.

Mondrian wrote : 'That which is immutable is above all misery and happiness : it is balance. By the immutable within us we are identified with all existence ; the mutable destroys our balance, limits us and separates us from all that is other than ourselves.'

Jaffé has drawn attention to the influence of the Dutch mystical thinker Dr Schoenmaekers. Both Mondrian and van der Leck lived at Laren near Amsterdam in 1916 (when the idea of De Stijl was being discussed). Schoenmaekers lived in Laren and apparently Mondrian and he saw each other frequently and had long discussions. Schoenmaekers published two books about this time : *The*

New Image of the World in 1915, and *Principles of Plastic Mathematics* in 1916.

The terminology in Mondrian's own writings seems to owe a lot to Schoenmaekers, but Jaffé's claim that Schoenmaekers' philosophy was one of the most important constituents in De Stijl is hardly substantiated. Schoenmakers' ideas seem to have been somewhat vague and his references, for instance, to line (horizontal = female, vertical = male, etc) and primary colours (blue receding, yellow advancing, red 'hovering'), although paralleled in Mondrian's writings, were common in aesthetic theory of the nineteenth and early twentieth centuries.

Undoubtedly some of Schoenmaekers' statements (quoted by Jaffé) are similar to those of Mondrian and even van Doesburg: 'We want to penetrate nature in such a way that the inner construction of reality is revealed to us.' (Schoenmaekers). Schoenmaekers puts great stress on 'relations' rather than things as do the De Stijl artists. But again, as with line and colour, this kind of thinking was more or less common property at the time.

Schoenmaekers defined style: 'Style in art is: the general in spite of the particular. By style, art is integrated in general, cultural life.'

Jaffé suggests that van Doesburg was influenced by Schoenmaekers in naming the magazine *De Stijl* (rather than *The Straight Line*). But van Doesburg does not appear to have been much influenced by Schoenmaekers at all. His ideas are mainly derived from nineteenth-century German philosophy and aesthetics in which he was well read. The architectural historian Reyner Banham's suggestion that van Doesburg's adoption of the name *De Stijl* was 'Berlagian' seems more likely. Berlage's definition of Style: 'Unity in Plurality' is not unlike Schoenmaekers' later definition.

Although there are almost as many Catholics in Holland as Protestants (41% compared to 50%), the Catholics are concentrated in the province of Limburg and North Brabant in the south-east. In the western part of Holland, where the De Stijl artists were centred, traditional Dutch Calvinism is predominant. All the Dutch De Stijl artists came from strict Calvinist families.

on pages 40 *and* 41 **J.J.P.Oud** Kiefhoek housing estate, Rotterdam, 1925–9; aerial view

J.J.P.Oud Spangen housing estate, Rotterdam, 1918–19 (destroyed)

J.J.P.Oud Tusschendijken housing estate, Rotterdam, 1920 (destroyed)
42

The Calvinists interpreted the first commandment literally: 'Thou shalt not make unto thee any graven image.' De Stijl translated the religious proscription against the graven image into an aesthetic one. Van Doesburg wrote in *De Stijl* in 1918:

It is wrong to identify the essence of thought with contemplation, just as it is wrong with regard to contemplation, to identify it with sensual representation of nature. The latter is a conception of classical and Roman Catholic origin, against which Protestantism has gone to battle (iconoclasm).

Jaffé has pointed out that in Dutch there is only a single word *schoon* for both 'clean' and 'beautiful'.

The Dutch character is full of contradictions. Traditionally Calvinist and puritanical there is also a strangely tolerant side to the Dutch which is perhaps the result of the Spanish influence—the red light districts and homosexual social clubs of Amsterdam are the most extreme examples.

Although Holland is so densely populated and urban the Dutch still remain in some ways a peasant people. Family ties are strong. Yet the Dutch do not shut themselves away within the family circle. There always remains a certain openness. The Dutch have always liked large windows and in the cities they do not draw the curtains in the evenings. The neat front-rooms and potted plants inside the window are on view. The Dutch love light. The typical home is fitted with strip, wall and centre lights.

Holland was relatively late in industrializing, but towards the end of the nineteenth century this took place rapidly. There was a steadily increasing movement of population from the land to the towns, from agricultural employment to industrial. Particularly important was the rapid expansion of the port of Rotterdam and an influx of workers to man the docks and allied industries. The land which has been reclaimed from the sea has always been owned by the state and houses built on this land are leasehold.

Holland was the first country to introduce, in 1901, systematic legislation for the national organization of urban development. This meant that every ten years a revised general plan had to be drawn up for all towns with over 10,000 inhabitants. In the first decades of the twentieth century Holland was in the forefront in housing policy. One of the earliest schemes was Berlage's plan for middle-class housing in Amsterdam South. Oud's first blocks in Rotterdam, the Spangen and Tusschendijken estates (destroyed in the Second World War) were among the earliest large-scale schemes for low-cost working-class housing.

In one area of Rotterdam South, workers who had recently arrived from the country were housed in village-like communities of single storey terrace houses in an attempt to recreate the intimacy of rural life within an urban environment. The inspiration was probably English garden city planning, but the Rotterdam development seems better integrated into the town, less self-consciously cottagey. The most successful (and most urban) of these communities was Oud's Kiefhoek estate.

Dutch architecture has usually been on a more or less domestic scale. The marshy ground of Holland has, in the past, made large monumental buildings of stone impractical. Brick has been the traditional Dutch building material (brick, of course, was really the first *standardized* building material). In the seventeenth century many of the towns were rebuilt in the Dutch domestic style, a model of anonymous, systematic architecture which remains human and intimate. Only in the nineteenth century were there a few attempts to create a monumental style. In many ways the De Stijl reaction against this was a return to the Dutch tradition. Although in the early years of De Stijl, Oud and van Doesburg called for a monumental (rather than a decorative) architecture, the later De Stijl architecture, like the Schröder house or Oud's estates of the 'twenties, is anti-monumental.

Art Nouveau architecture and design was restrained and geometric in Holland, in contrast to the rich and florid Art Nouveau of Belgium. Only in the paintings and graphic work of the Dutch-Indonesian artist Jan Toorop, and to lesser extent that of Johan Thorn Prikker, are the wilder elements of Art Nouveau apparent in their rhythmical linear extravagance. There are slight Art Nouveau elements in Mondrian's work before 1911.

Nor did the Gothic revival take very extreme form in Dutch architecture. M.P.J.Cuypers' large, rather busy, brick public buildings in Amsterdam, like the Rijkmuseum and the Central Station, are typical of the Dutch architecture of the second half of the nineteenth century.

J.J.P.Oud Kiefhoek housing estate, Rotterdam, 1925–9

Berlage, who began as an eclectic, stripped his style down to simplified, sober Gothic and Renaissance forms. The design of his best known building, the Stock Exchange in Amsterdam, went through several versions from late Gothic and Renaissance styles

Jan Toorop *Three Brides* 1893
Mixed media Collection Rijksmuseum Kröller-Müller, Otterlo

H.P.Berlage Holland House, 1–4 Bury St, London E.C.3, 1914
(now slightly altered) Photo courtesy Brian Houden

to an austere, bare Romanesque. The façades became flat and two-dimensional. The wall is reduced to a plane surface and the dense surface characteristics of its material—brick—are emphasized.

Berlage's most advanced building is not in Holland, but an office block in London designed in 1914. The use of metal windows and the marked vertical and horizontal character of the fenestration is particularly interesting in the context of the development of De Stijl architecture a few years later. However, Berlage's influence on the next generation of Dutch architects was as much through his extensive writings as through his buildings.

46

Berlage insisted on the importance of the wall as a plane. No decoration must disguise it: 'before all else, the wall must be shown nude in all its sleek beauty. Anything fixed on it must be shunned as an embarrassment. Thus walling would receive its true value again in the sense that its nature as *plane* would remain'.

Architecture should achieve 'the creation of space, not the sketching of façades'. Berlage described how this was to be done: 'A spatial envelope is established by means of walls, whereby a space, a series of spaces is manifested, according to the complexity of the walling.'

Berlage emphasized the importance of geometry and mathematics in the creation of form in the visual arts, as in music. He advocated the use of proportional systems in design which would create an effect of repose and balance and hence Style, in contrast to the restless quality of nineteenth-century eclecticism. Berlage believed that architecture should absorb painting and sculpture into a kind of *Gesamtkunstwerk* (Total Work of Art) and that interest in the applied arts would grow at the expense of the fine arts.

Like Morris, Berlage was a socialist, but a free-thinking rationalist, not a Christian socialist. It is ironic that just as Morris's expensive handwork was bought only by the wealthy, so Berlage's best known work is the Amsterdam Stock Exchange building.

Van der Leck was a life-long socialist and the writings of most of the artists and architects associated with De Stijl were inspired by left-wing ideals. In contrast to Berlage's almost positivist viewpoint they laid stress on the importance of spiritual values. Van Doesburg wrote in *De Stijl* in 1923:

The artist is neither a proletarian nor a bourgeois and what he creates belongs neither to the proletariat nor to the bourgeoisie. It belongs to everyone. Art is a spiritual activity in man, with the aim to deliver him from the chaos of life, from tragedy. Art is free in the application of its means, but bound by its own laws and by nothing but its laws.

P.J.Klaarhamer Buffet, 1915
Made for Klaarhamer by Rietveld

P.J.Klaarhamer Chair, 1915
Made for Klaarhamer by Rietveld

Although he was not directly associated with De Stijl the career of
the Utrecht architect and designer, P.J.Klaarhamer, is important in
relation to De Stijl. Van der Leck collaborated with Klaarhamer on
illustrations to the *Song of Songs* as early as 1905, and again in
1918 in designs for the stands for Messrs Bruynzeel at the Utrecht

Gerrit Rietveld Chair, 1908

Fair. Between 1911 and 1915 Rietveld took an evening course in architecture under Klaarhamer and through him he met van der Leck. In 1915 while working for Klaarhamer, Rietveld built several pieces of furniture designed by Klaarhamer in the simplified tradition of the Dutch Arts and Crafts style.

51

Van der Mey Scheepvaartshuis, Amsterdam, 1911–15
De Klerk and Kramer worked on the detailing and interior. Photograph, the author

With Frank Lloyd Wright, Berlage was the most important influence on Dutch architecture during the 1910s and his influence persisted, in the work of the Amsterdam School, until the early 'twenties. The exuberant forms of many of the buildings of the Amsterdam School might perhaps be considered as a late flowering of Art Nouveau in Dutch architecture, although the school is often linked with the so-called Expressionist style in German architecture of this period (early Mendelsohn, Poelzig, etc) and in certain ways anticipates the decorative style of the 'twenties and 'thirties.

Michel de Klerk Zaanstraat housing estate, 1917–21
Photograph, the author

Michel de Klerk Zaanstraat housing estate, 1917–21

The earliest building in the Amsterdam Style is the Scheepvaar-thuis (Shipping House), a concrete-framed structure concealed beneath jutting sculpture and decorative brickwork. The most imaginative work of the Amsterdam School is Michel de Klerk's housing estate along the Zaanstraat, where soft brick and tile-hung forms contrasted with sharp, angular windows hint at Zeppelins and rockets.

J.A.Brinkman and **L.C. van der Vlugt** Van Nelle factory,
Van Nelleweg, Rotterdam, 1928. Photograph, Brian Housden

The De Stijl artists and architects, particularly van Doesburg and Oud, regarded the Amsterdam School as the enemy on the doorstep. It was the butt of continual attacks from them in the *De Stijl* magazine and elsewhere. (They usually singled out the most extreme examples, like a house designed in the shape of a tram!) Yet at its best, in the work of architects like Piet Kramer and de Klerk, the Amsterdam Style was arguably just as valid and modern as the Rotterdam Style exemplified by Oud's cool, anonymous white housing estates of the 'twenties or the van Nelle factory (outside Rotterdam).

The German architect Erich Mendelsohn, invited by the Amsterdam School to visit Holland, wrote back to his wife:

Oud is functional so as to talk with Gropius. Amsterdam is dynamic . . . The first sets ratio before everything: perception through analysis. The second sets perception through vision. Analytical Rotterdam refuses vision; visionary Amsterdam does not understand cold objectivity . . . If Amsterdam goes a step further towards reason and Rotterdam's blood does not freeze, then they may unite. Otherwise Rotterdam will pursue the way of mere construction with deathly chill in its veins and Amsterdam will be destroyed by the fire of its own dynamism.

What Mendelsohn foresaw more or less came about. The Rotterdam School was absorbed into the International Style and debased, the Amsterdam School barely survived de Klerk's death in 1923. What generally emerged in Dutch architecture in the 'twenties and 'thirties was a combination of formal elements from early De Stijl architecture with a use of traditional Dutch brickwork derived from the Amsterdam School, as in the work of W.M.Dudok and J.F.Staal. Dudok's Hilversum town hall became widely influential in Europe between the wars and was much imitated.

3 De Stijl: development and ideals

The examples and illustrations in the last two chapters are given as visual parallels and precursors rather than as necessarily direct influences. Art historians are fond of the 'billiard ball' theory of influence and transference of ideas. A does this, B gets to hear about it or sees the work and then does this, C sees it and does this, and so on. This is a naïve view of the history of ideas.

The history of science, for instance, shows many examples of two scientists, who have no contact, coming up with the same or similar theories at approximately the same time, often only discovering the ideas of the other at some later date. This happens too in the arts; and particularly in the visual arts. When one man learns of what another has been working on in a similar direction this may confirm him in the way he is going, not influence him directly. This seems to have been the case with the inter-relation between the painters associated with De Stijl and between these painters and architects and designers. This is not to deny that there was probably *some* direct influence from one artist or architect to another at various points in the development of De Stijl.

One of the most important factors in the development of De Stijl was the neutrality of Holland during the First World War. Looking back in 1929 van Doesburg wrote in a Swiss periodical:

We all lived in the spirit of a genesis. Though there was no war in our neutral Netherlands, yet the war outside caused commotion and a spiritual tension; the soil was nowhere as propitious for the gathering of renewing forces. The war, raging at our borders, drove home many artists who had been working abroad.

Van t'Hoff who had been working for two years in architectural offices in America (including Wright's) returned to Holland. Van der Leck hurried home from a trip to Morocco. Mondrian, who had come from Paris to visit his father who was ill, was forced to remain in Holland for the duration of the war. Vantongerloo came to the Hague as a refugee from Belgium.

In the last (memorial) number of *De Stijl* in 1932 Mondrian wrote:

It was a sombre and painful time, the time of the Great War, in Holland as well. Due to the international understanding between

Piet Mondrian *Composition in Grey, Red, Yellow and Blue* 1920
Oil. Collection Tate Gallery, London

Furniture by **Gerrit Rietveld**. *At back, left,* buffet, 1919; *right,* Berlin chair,
1923. *Middle, left to right:* military chair with arms, 1923; military stool,
1923; child's toy wheel-barrow, 1920; red-blue armchair, 1917–18. *Front,
left,* chair with arms, 1919; *right,* end table, 1923
Collection Mr and Mrs Brian Housden

peoples, as much as to our human and artistic sensibility, the depression and anguish of war extended inevitably there where no fighting occurred. In spite of everything, in Holland there still existed the possibility of being preoccupied with purely ethical questions. Thus art continued there, developed there and what is particularly remarkable, is that it was only possible for it to continue in the same way as before the war; that is to say moving towards an abstract expression.

Only in neutral Switzerland (Dadaism) and revolutionary Russia (Suprematism and Constructivism) was there a similar co-operative development at this time. These three movements: De Stijl, Constructivism and Dadaism, were later to come together and interact during the early 'twenties in a way which determined the subsequent development of twentieth-century art, architecture and design.

As well as bringing together the artists and giving them time while the rest of Europe was at war, the neutrality of Holland helped to give Dutch architects the initiative in combining and developing the new ideas in architecture that had come out of Europe and America in the first decade of the twentieth century. As a result Holland led Europe for a short period in the early 'twenties.

In 1924, in the French architectural magazine, *L'Architecture Vivante*, the editor Jean Badovici wrote:

Today, Holland seems to be the country richest in architectural activity, the one which must be named as exercising the predominant influence. One cannot but be astonished, when one sees this country, where individualists are so conspicuous and often so opposed, give birth to an art of so beautiful a unity. The most diverse individualists there have grouped themselves together and co-ordinated their efforts, to work in an harmonious collaboration towards the development and beauty of the cities.

Yet within a few years Germany was to make good the time lag of the war and take the lead in the late 'twenties.

Theo van Doesburg was born in Utrecht in 1883. (Rietveld and van der Leck also came from Utrecht.) His real name was Christiaan Emil Marie Küpper and he adopted the name of van Doesburg early on in his career as an artist. Later he was to invent two more pseudonyms under which to publish his Dadaist poems and essays in *De Stijl* and elsewhere: a Dutch alter ego, I.K.Bonset, and an Italian, Aldo Camini.

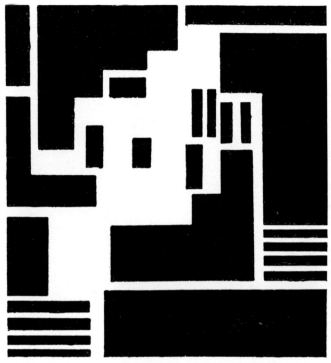

Design used for the cover of the early issues of *De Stijl*, based on the painting by Vilmos Huszar (see page 10)

The Küpper family seems to have been fairly well off and van Doesburg had some private means with which he was later able to finance the printing and publishing of the *De Stijl* magazine. Van Doesburg began to study painting in 1899 when he was sixteen. In 1908, at the age of twenty-five, he held his first exhibition at the Hague. From 1912 he contributed art criticism and essays to various Dutch periodicals and magazines, in particular *Eenheid*, a recently founded progressive review.

At the outbreak of war, van Doesburg was conscripted and stationed with the Dutch Frontier Guard on the Belgian border. It was during this period of military service that he seems to have conceived of the idea of a group or association of artists and architects

ABONNEMENT BIJ VOORUITBETALING BINNENLAND 4.50 BUITENLAND 5.50 PER JAARGANG. VOOR ANNONCES WENDE MEN ZICH TOT DEN UITGEVER.

ADRES VAN REDACTIE: KORT GALGEWATER 3 LEIDEN. ADMINISTRATIE: X. HARMS TIEPEN, HYPOLITUSBUURT 37 DELFT, INTERC. TEL. 729 EN 690.

MAANDBLAD VOOR DE BEELDENDE VAKKEN. REDACTIE THEO VAN DOESBURG. UITGAVE X. HARMS TIEPEN.

1e JAARGANG.   APRIL NEGENTIENHONDERDACHTTIEN.   NUMMER 6.

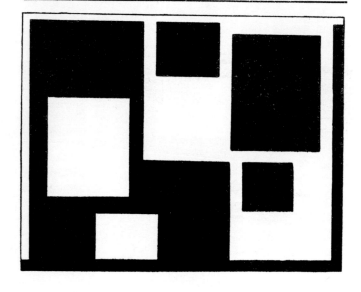

Logotype used in early issues of *De Stijl*
Composition **Vilmos Huszar**
From *De Stijl,* 1918 (Vol 1 no. 6)

and a periodical in which they could express their views. Here too he met the poet and essayist Antony Kok, who was to be one of the founder members of *De Stijl*. Kok seems to have further stimulated van Doesburg's interest in literature (during the 'twenties he wrote many poems and published a novel), although apparently van Doesburg had already written poems under the influence of the Italian Futurist, Marinetti, in 1913.

Van Doesburg had contacted Oud and Mondrian in 1915, and when he was demobbed in 1916 he settled in Leiden where Oud was also living at the time. Van Doesburg discussed the idea of a magazine and a group with Oud and the Hungarian painter and designer Huszar, who lived nearby at Voorburg. Early in 1917 van Doesburg visited Mondrian and van der Leck who were both living at Laren, near Amsterdam, and tried to enlist their support—van Doesburg had for some time been an admirer of Mondrian's work. Both Mondrian and van der Leck seem to have been initially a bit wary of van Doesburg's idea of a group containing architects as well. Jaffé quotes part of a letter from Mondrian to van Doesburg written in February 1917: 'You should remember that my things are still intended to be painting, that is to say, they are plastic representation, in and by themselves, not part of a building. Furthermore, they have been made in a small room.' Van der Leck feared that the architects would dominate the painters and, apparently under the impression that this was happening, disassociated himself from De Stijl a year later. However, van der Leck was prepared to collaborate with architects providing it was an equal partnership, and in the same year that he left De Stijl (1918) worked with the architect Klaarhamer on the interior design for a stand at the Utrecht Fair.

However, as van Doesburg was later to point out in many essays, he believed that the different visual arts, painting, sculpture, architecture must, at the beginning at least, be clearly separated so that they could individually purify their means of expression.

In his magazine articles (1912–14) van Doesburg had laid the theoretical foundations of what was to become De Stijl, insisting on the need for the straight line and the rectangular principle, and calling for a renewal of spiritual values in art. Between 1914 and 1916 he was able to paint little himself while in the army, but seems to have had time enough to develop his ideas.

Piet Mondrian *Composition in Black and White* 1917
Oil. Collection Rijksmuseum Kröller-Müller, Otterlo

After van Doesburg left the army in mid-1916 and began to come into closer contact with Mondrian it is difficult to determine their exact relationship, as for the years 1916 to 1920 the documentation and chronology of the work of both painters is far from satisfactory. It seems that by 1917 they had arrived at approximately the same point; Mondrian in practice, van Doesburg in ideas. Van Doesburg encouraged Mondrian to put his own ideas into words and once out of the army found himself able to develop his own ideas in terms of actual paintings.

64

Piet Mondrian *Self-portrait* 1918
Oil. Loan S.B. Slijper. Collection Haags Gemeentemuseum, The Hague

Theo van Doesburg *The Cow* 1917
Oil. Collection Museum of Modern Art, New York

Mondrian's major contribution to the initial development of De Stijl was the series of 'plus and minus' paintings from 1914 to 1917. These are sometimes known also as 'pier and ocean' paintings because they were inspired by the sea and pier at Scheveningen, near the Hague ('Observing sea, sky and stars, I sought to indicate their plastic function through a multiplicity of crossing verticals and horizontals').

In his book *Principles of Neo-Plasticism* published at the Bauhaus in 1925, but based on essays written around 1917, van Doesburg sees the expressive means of all the arts as the relationships between positive and negative elements. In music, sounds (positive) and silence (negative); in painting, colour (positive) and non-colour—black, white or grey—(negative); in architecture, plane and mass (positive) and space (negative); in sculpture, volume (positive) and space (negative).

In *The Cow* (1917) van Doesburg made his most important early contribution to the stylistic development of De Stijl, the introduction of a strong asymmetricality. Mondrian, whose use of

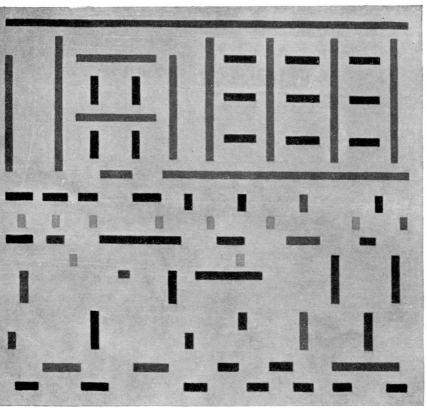

Bart van der Leck *Geometrical Composition* 1917
Oil. Collection Rijksmuseum Kröller-Müller, Otterlo

asymmetricality had been confined to small areas of a more or less all-over surface coverage (in the 'plus and minus' paintings) was to adopt this strong asymmetricality in his own work, particularly from 1921.

Although Mondrian had avoided the use of green in his earlier paintings and had used primary colour much reduced with white to pale tints for some time, the introduction of pure primary colour used in full saturation was one of van der Leck's three important

Bart van der Leck *Composition* 1919
Oil. Collection Kröller-Müller, Otterlo

Bart van der Leck *Beggars* 1914
Tempera. Loan Mrs S.S. van der Meulen. Collection Haags
Gemeentemuseum, The Hague

contributions to De Stijl. In the letter from Mondrian to van Doesburg, already quoted, Mondrian writes (February 1917): 'I use
subdued colours for the time being, adapting myself to the present
surroundings and to the outer world; this does not mean that I
should not prefer a purer colouring. Otherwise you might think that
I contradict myself in my work.' Mondrian doesn't seem to have
used primary colour in full saturation until 1921.

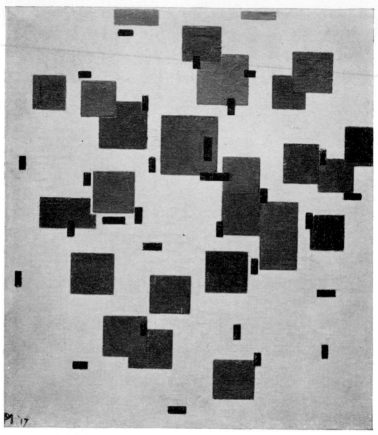

Piet Mondrian *Composition in Blue A* 1917
Oil. Collection Rijksmuseum Kröller-Müller, Otterlo

Theo van Doesburg *Rhythm of a Russian Dance* 1918
Oil. Collection Musuem of Modern Art, New York

The second important contribution of van der Leck to De Stijl was the use of discretely separated elements in his painting, neither crossing nor intersecting. Thus his *Composition* (see page 67) in the Kröller-Müller museum is a carefully ordered composition of thin rectangles of primary colour of uniform width but differing length. It looks rather like the plan of the carefully-sawn wooden members of a piece of Rietveld furniture—the red-blue chair for instance—laid out ready for assembly. Although entirely abstract it is quite likely that this painting was originally derived from an

70

Piet Mondrian *Composition with Coloured Planes No. 3,* 1917
Collection Haags Gemeentemuseum, The Hague

analysis of a cow, like van Doesburg's painting. This is clearer in
the second version of this *Composition* that van der Leck painted.

Van der Leck's third important contribution was the insistence
on the absolute flatness of his planes of colour, as Mondrian ac-
knowledged in the final (van Doesburg memorial) issue of *De Stijl*
in 1932: '. . . van der Leck, who, though still figurative, painted
in compact planes of pure colour. My more or less Cubist technique—in consequence still more or less picturesque—underwent
the influence of his exact technique.'

Although van Doesburg usually worked with primary colours he
often used green throughout his career (in the Aubette decorations
in 1927 for instance). One of his best paintings *Composition 17* of
1919 (see illustration page 111) is predominantly green.

72

Piet Mondrian *Composition, Checkerboard, Bright Colours* 1919
Oil. Collection Haags Gemeentemuseum, The Hague

In 1918, in *Rhythm of a Russian Dance* (see page 71) van Doesburg uses tinted colours in thin rectangles of colour separated from
one another in a way slightly similar to van der Leck's *Composition*
of 1917, but composed so that a pulsating optical rhythm is created
rather than the calculated balance of van der Leck's work.

Whereas van der Leck's *Composition* is flat and planar, Mondrian's *Composition in Blue A* (see page 70) creates a remarkable sense of simulated space, close to the definition and explora-
tion of real space in Rietveld's chair, although not so carefully
worked out in these terms as his paintings of the late 'thirties (see
page 13). This composition contains the seeds of virtually all Mondrian's later works, including his last 'boogie-woogie' paintings
done shortly before his death in New York.

In 1919 both van Doesburg and Mondrian began to divide their canvases into small squares which were then used as the modules for asymmetric compositions. (Van Doesburg's tiled floor for the interior of Oud's sanatorium 'De Vonk' at Noordwijkerhout was based on this system.) As Alred H.Barr has pointed out in his pamphlet on De Stijl, this is anticipated by traditional Dutch tiling (or one might add, Dutch decorative brickwork) which could have been a direct influence on De Stijl painting. In 1920 Mondrian adopted a rather freer style of arranging flat rectangles of subdued primary colour and greys, whereas van Doesburg continued with his modular compositions until his introduction of the diagonal around 1924.

J.J.P.Oud and **Theo van Doesburg** 'De Vonk',
Noorwijkerhout, 1917–18
Van Doesburg collaborated with Oud on the interior and designed the geometrically patterned floor

Theo van Doesburg *Composition IX* 1917
Oil. Collection Haags Gemeentemuseum, The Hague

Vilmos Huszar *Composition* 1918
Lithograph. Collection Rijksmuseum Kröller-Müller, Otterlo

76

Gerrit Rietveld Child's chair, 1919
From *De Stijl* 1919

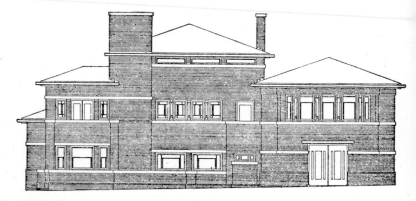

Jan Wils Hotel De Dubbele Sleutel, Woerden, 1919
Drawing from *De Stijl* 1919

Robert van t'Hoff Villa at Huis ter Heide, near Utrecht
Drawings from *De Stijl* 1919

In 1916 Robert van t'Hoff had built two villas at Huis ter Heide near Utrecht. The larger and more important house is quite obviously directly inspired by Wright's work and by one building by Wright in particular, the Unity Chapel in Chicago. Although very obviously designed under the influence of Wright, van t'Hoff's villa, one of the first to have been built by the concrete post and slab technique, translates Wright into a distinctly European idiom. The glazed corner of the window next to the porch for instance is closer to Gropius' Fagus factory (see page 22) than to Wright and the whole exterior is less mannered than Wright, its outlines more precise.

Jan Wils restaurant 'De Dubbele Sleutel' of three years later is also extremely influenced by Wright in the use of brick, steps, roofs and cornering. Wils' Papaverhof estate of the following year (1920) has moved several steps onwards towards the European modern style, although one or two Wrightian elements are retained.

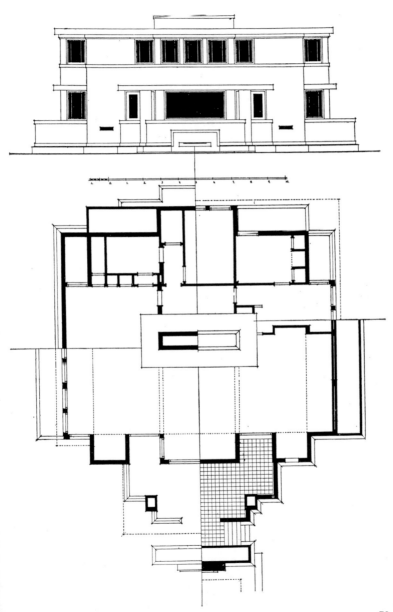

Oud's designs for a row of houses above the beach at Scheveningen (1917) were never executed. Like van t'Hoff's villa they are still symmetrical, although stark and stripped down. Oud himself described them as inspired by Cubism, but there is really nothing Cubist about them. The design is plain, yet ingenious, based on a system of interlocking cubic volumes that seems derived from purely architectural thinking, not by way of painting.

If there seems a slight resemblance between Oud's esplanade houses and the paintings of van Doesburg, Mondrian or van der Leck of the same period (other than a simplification of means), this is probably because the scheme exists only in careful drawings and a pristine white model with 'blind' white windows and doors. Oud's presentation techniques may have owed something to the

J.J.P.Oud Model for apartment houses on an esplanade above a beach at Scheveningen, 1917 (not executed)

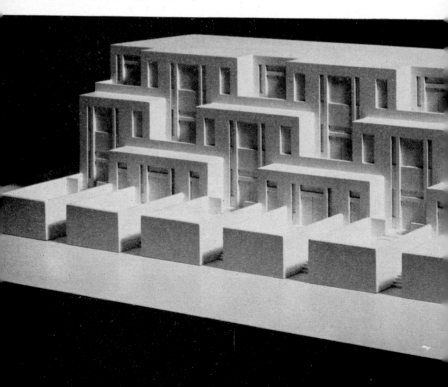

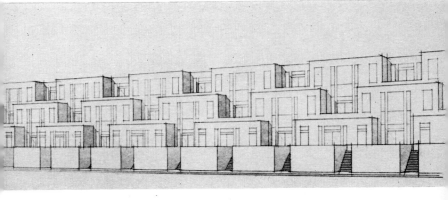

J.J.P.Oud Design for apartment houses on an esplanade above a beach at Scheveningen, 1917 (not executed)

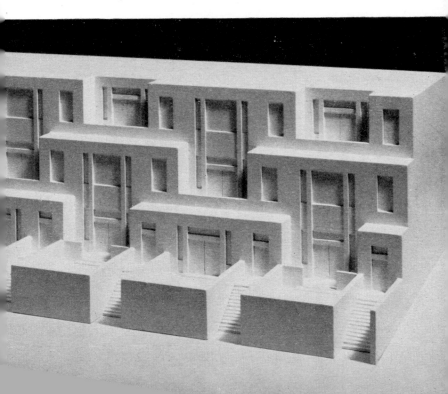

Georges Vantongerloo *Relation of Volumes* 1919
Courtesy Marlborough Gallery, London

J.J.P.Oud Model for factory with office at Purmerend,
1919 (not executed)

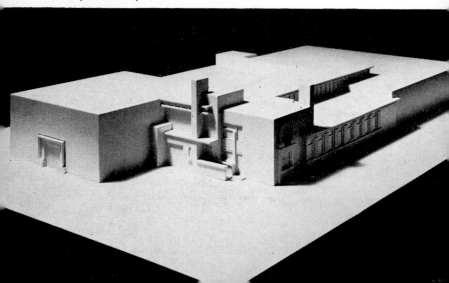

painting of De Stijl or the sculpture of Vantongerloo, but not his architectural ideas.

The visual parallel between Oud's design for a factory at Purmerend (1919)—also not built and extant only in careful drawings and a model—and Vantongerloo's sculptures is much closer, although this is only true of the central part of the design where vertical and horizontal elements cross and intersect in a kind of nuclear structure. But like most of Oud's work it is essentially a surface composition, rather than a space composition, a manipulation of a façade. The other parts of the design are less interesting, more obviously Wrightian, except for the interpenetration of different volumes as represented by the intersection of roof levels. Again the fact that the design exists only in drawings and models tends to exaggerate its sculptural qualities.

Some of Vantongerloo's earliest sculptural constructions, made when he was living at the Hague in 1917, are based on the sphere rather than the cube and even when his work looks purely cubic, the definition of a spherical volume is often hinted at.

The first issue of *De Stijl* is dated October 1917 but the First Manifesto of De Stijl was not published in the magazine until November 1918: this was signed by van Doesburg, van t'Hoff, Huszar, Kok, Mondrian, Vantongerloo and Wils and printed in Dutch, German, English and French. Van der Leck had already left by this time and Oud, who was appointed City Architect of Rotterdam in 1918, seems not to have signed out of professional caution.

The manifesto was obviously intended to make sympathizers abroad aware of what was happening in Holland and also to extend the movement onto an international basis. In an article published in a Swiss magazine in 1929 van Doesburg wrote: 'As the World War was coming to an end, we all came to feel the need of securing an interest in our efforts beyond the narrow boundaries of Holland.' Mondrian returned to Paris and van Doesburg began to travel around Europe making contacts with artists and particularly architects abroad. After the War many of the artists and architects (mainly Dutch) who had earlier been associated with De Stijl severed their connection, and to replace them van Doesburg invited some of those whom he had made contact with abroad to join the movement, like the Russian Constructivist El Lissitzky, the German

Cover, *De Stijl* 1921

ex-Dadaist maker of abstract films, Hans Richter, the Austrian designer Frederik Kiesler and the ex-Bauhaus student Werner Graeff.
The only important new Dutch member was the young architect
and town planner Cornelis van Eesteren. Other new members
were the Dutch painter Cesar Domela and the German painter
Friedel Vordemberge-Gildewart.

The change towards a more international outlook is symbolized
by the changes in format and layout of the magazine in 1921. The
format is changed from a small pocket-shape to a wide 'landscape'
shape with a double column of print. The layout and typography
become purer and simplified, less Dutch in origin, in line with the
internationalism of the New Typography.

The origins of the New Typography are diverse. It appears as a
fully formed style in Russia, Holland and Germany in the early
'twenties. In an essay on the book published in 1927, Lissitzky

154

Page from *De Stijl* 1921

traces the development of the New Typography back to Marinetti, Wyndham Lewis's layout for BLAST in 1914 and the Dadaist photo-montageur John Heartfield's layout of the magazine *Neue Jugend*, edited by his brother Helmut Herzfeld in 1917. What is certain is that these different elements fused together about 1920–21. Van Doesburg's and Lissitzky's first typographical designs in the new style seem to have been approximately contemporaneous (Lissitzky and van Doesburg did not meet until 1922), but as there is a marked change in the *De Stijl* typography after van Doesburg's visits abroad in 1920–21 it may well be that the change was the result of work he had seen in Germany or elsewhere; it can, however, also be seen as a purification of the original layout for *De Stijl*. At any rate it seems certain that both Lissitzky and van Doesburg were practising the New Typography before it was introduced at the Bauhaus by Moholy-Nagy—in 1923.

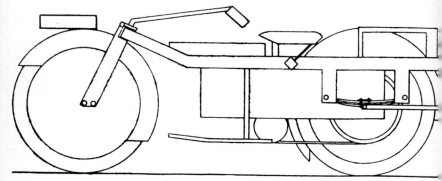

Werner Graeff Design for a motorbike
From *De Stijl* 1922

Increasingly in its international phase the *De Stijl* magazine became a vehicle and voice for whatever van Doesburg considered
important. Van Doesburg travelled through Europe in the 'twenties,
proselytizing for De Stijl in Berlin, in Weimar (at the Bauhaus), in
Prague and in Paris. Although he spread the Style abroad he also
absorbed other styles and activities seemingly at odds with the
original ideas of De Stijl into the pages of the magazine. Dadaism

Vilmos Huszar Advertising kiosk
From *De Stijl* 1927 (Jubilee number)

(particularly Dadaist poetry), Russian Constructivism and the 'tough' school of Berlin abstraction were all given space. Yet although this may have upset purists like Mondrian and others of the original members of De Stijl, van Doesburg's inclusiveness wasn't really contradictory, and his ability to reconcile such seemingly opposed manifestations as geometric abstraction and Dadaism was one of the formative achievements of the 'twenties.

Vordemberge-Gildewart *Composition*
Collection Stedelijk Museum, Amsterdam

88

Cesar Domela *Composition* 1924
Oil. Collection Stedelijk Museum, Amsterdam

Ideals

In *De Stijl* in 1918 van Doesburg wrote:

Pure thought, in which no image based on phenomena is involved, but where numbers, measurement, relations and abstract line have occupied its place, manifests itself by way of the idea, as reasonableness in Chinese, Greek and German philosophy and in the form of beauty in the Neo-plasticism of our time.

Neo-plasticism, or new plasticism (*nieuwe beelding*) was the term originally adopted by Mondrian from Dr Schoenmaekers to describe the qualities the De Stijl artists were striving for. The opposite of Neo-plasticism in van Doesburg's terminology is Neo- or modern baroque (as exemplified in architecture by the Amsterdam School).

In the first issue of the *De Stijl* magazine in 1917 van Doesburg wrote in his introduction:

As soon as the artists in the various branches of plastic art will have realized that they must speak a universal language, they will no longer cling to their individuality with such anxiety. They will serve a general principle far beyond the limitations of individuality. By serving the general principle they will be made to produce, of their own accord, an organic style ... Only by consistently following this principle can the new plastic beauty manifest itself in all objects as a style, born from a new relationship between the artist and society.

Van Doesburg writes in *De Stijl* in 1920 that the scientific discoveries and beliefs of an age are reflected in its art; yet, in fact, the insistence on the straight line and the rectangle seems not to have been so much a reflection of discoveries in science or even advances in technology as a common feeling among the artists and architects that certain forms were appropriate for architecture, sculpture and painting in the new era of the First World War and its aftermath, a kind of visual cleansing, a rejection of the decorative luxuriance of the immediately preceding style, Art Nouveau.

Looking back in an article published in an English little magazine *Ray* in 1927 van Doesburg wrote: 'To construct ... *without any illusion*, without any decoration, is one of the principal aims of the *Stijl* movement.'

Painting must be abstract, architecture should be unadorned and reveal the construction and the function. Oud, in various essays, also pronounces strongly against decoration. Yet the use of the advancing and receding characteristics of the primary colours, which creates illusion, which might even be called decorative, is permitted.

In an article in *De Stijl* of 1922 Mondrian makes a distinction between the new and *the* new. In the past the old has always at some time been new; but *the* new is different. Mondrian sees man at the turning-point of civilization. Everything old is finished. The separation between the old and *the* new is 'absolute and definite'. It was this sense of *the* new that the De Stijl artists and architects wanted to express, the qualities of living in the twentieth century—that made it totally different from the nineteenth century. Hence soft forms which had a stylistic relation to Art Nouveau, like those of de Klerk and the Amsterdam School had to be rejected and attacked.

In his *Ray* article van Doesburg wrote:

Architecture, the synthesis of all the arts, will spring from the human function, simply from life, and not as formerly from types already created by ancient people who had an entirely different manner of living, different customs and habits, and who thought in a manner totally different to our way of thought.

In other words, architecture had to change to fit the newness of twentieth-century life, as had Rietveld's Schröder house with its sliding partitions—a flexible space designed to suit the new informality and flexibility of modern living. Either openness or closedness are available, the social and the private, or in De Stijl terminology, the universal and the individual: 'The new art has brought forward what the new consciousness of time contains: a balance between the universal and the individual.' ('First Manifesto', *De Stijl*, 1918)

Writing in 1918, Oud sees a direct connection between art and the social development of the age and sees a parallel with De Stijl faith in the universal and abstract in the urge to organize individuals into 'groups, unions, leagues, societies, trusts, monopolies etc'; 'This reconciliation of spiritual and social striving, a necessary for achieving culture, forms the foundation for style.' He sees the spirit of the times expressing itself in machine- rather than hand-production which reaches only a few rich individuals.

Oud sees the mistake of Ruskin and Morris in that they believed machine-production capable only of inferior imitations of handicrafts and in rejecting the idea of techniques specifically designed for machine-production. Oud believes that the development of machine techniques has resulted in 'pure form'. He writes that 'the emergence of purity always has aesthetic consequences' and : 'That the pure application of machine methods of production leads to aesthetic results is already proven in : buildings, well-designed books (printed by machine), textiles, etc.'

Oud ignores the fact that perhaps the first *style* designed or evolved specifically for machine-production and in response to modern technology (for instance, the electric light) had been Art Nouveau, which was not at all 'pure' in form.

In an article on Wright in *De Stijl* (1918), Oud says the outside of the building should make clear what goes on inside : 'The organization of the activities in a building leads to one of the distinguishing features of pure architecture : the expression of this organization on the outside of the building through a conscious grouping of the masses.' Oud doesn't recognize, however, that the functions of a building may change and that therefore the grouping of the masses of the exterior to express the conceived function of the building may be unnecessarily rigid. This is why the exterior of Rietveld's Schröder house does not 'express' the function of the interior, except insofar as its seemingly unconnected planes suggest the flexible nature of the interior.

Mondrian is more idealistic than Oud, one might say in the light of subsequent events in the 'thirties, less realistic, seeing contemporary social developments towards the universal and collective rather than the individual as a move in the direction of socialism or syndicalism : 'Autocracy, imperialism with its (natural) law of the strongest, is about to collapse—if it has not done so already—giving way to the spiritual powers of law.' (*De Stijl*, 1918) Oud, however, had seen that the same tendency to produce unions, leagues and societies also produced trusts and monopolies.

Van t'Hoff sees the machine and mechanized building methods as ways of improving the workman's lot : 'We demand a maximum of labour from the machine, a minimum from the workman who should not be in the least concerned about the personal feelings of the designer.' (*De Stijl*, 1918)

And as late as 1931, in an essay written shortly before his death, van Doesburg wrote: 'Under the supremacy of materialism, handicrafts reduced men to the level of machines; the proper tendency for the machine (in the sense of cultural development) is the unique medium of the very opposite, social liberation.'

In the same essay (and earlier during the 'twenties), van Doesburg spoke of the machine as a 'phenomenon of spiritual discipline'. Shortly afterwards, the autocracy that Mondrian had thought to be on the verge of collapse harnessed the 'phenomenon of spiritual discipline' to its own destructive and materialist ends.

In his first article in *De Stijl* (1917), Mondrian sees the trend towards an abstract life reflected in trends in interior decoration, in fashion and even in the dance. (Despite being a reclusive bachelor, he remained into old age a great dancer.) He sees the tango replacing the waltz—straight lines replacing rounded movements.

Mondrian writes of the metropolis as the embodiment of abstract life, where nature has been 'straightened out'. He welcomes the increasing engulfment of the countryside by the city, rectifying nature's 'capriciousness' (*De Stijl* 1919, 1922, 1924). Later in life he hated even natural greenery, several times when dining with friends in Paris asking to be seated so that he didn't have to look out of the window at the green trees. He was never happier than when in New York during the last years of his life.

In an essay of 1927 Vantongerloo pointed out that nature as we see it today was not really nature at all, but man-made, or at least man-controlled nature. The merciless jungle was nature in its natural state. In a later essay he pointed out that in technological advances, like the development of the aeroplane, man does not follow nature (i.e. the flight of the bird) but devises his own methods.

In 1927 Mondrian wrote in the magazine that in the future man 'will select his own surroundings and create them. He will therefore not regret the lack of nature, as the masses do, who have been forced in spite of themselves to leave it . . . He will build cities, hygienic and beautiful, by a balanced contrast of buildings, constructions and empty spaces. Then he will be quite as happy indoors as outdoors.'

For Rietveld the purpose of art, architecture and design, as of all other worthwhile human endeavour, was to temper nature by bringing it into a human scale: 'We must not consider the human scale which in our field is so highly praised, as a cultural attainment. Because in principle we must bring things into a human scale, in contrast with the inhuman in nature, as a means of self-preservation. This tendency is universal.'

In *De Stijl* in 1923 a manifesto appeared over the signatures of van Doesburg and van Eesteren, 'Toward a Collective Construction', in which art is seen as a means of controlling the environment, or perhaps constructing an entirely *art*ificial environment. Once the environment is constructed there will no longer be any need for art, except perhaps to adjust the environment according to changing needs. Like Dada, De Stijl resolves itself to the elimination of art.

In 1926 van Doesburg published a manifesto in English in *De Stijl* entitled 'The End of Art':

One cannot renew Art. 'Art' is an invention of the Renaissance which has today refined itself to the utmost degree possible. An enormous concentration was needed to make good works of Art. One could only develop this concentration by neglecting life (as in religion) or to lose life entirely. That is today impossible for we are only interested in life !

We too must distribute our forces upon all life. That is real progress. This progress negates exclusive concentration. It can only give instantaneous snapshots of life. That is the first reason why Art is impossible.

. . . Let's refresh ourselves with things that are not Art : the bathroom, the W.C., the bathtub, the telescope, the bicycle, the auto, the subways, the flat-iron. There are many people who know how to make such good unartistic things. But they are hindered, and their movements are dictated, by the priests of Art. Art, whose function nobody knows, hinders the function of life. For the sake of progress we must destroy Art. Because the function of modern life is stronger than Art, every attempt to renew Art (Futurism, Cubism, Expressionism) failed. They are all bankrupt. Let us not waste our time with them. Let us rather create a new life-form which is adequate to the functioning of modern life.

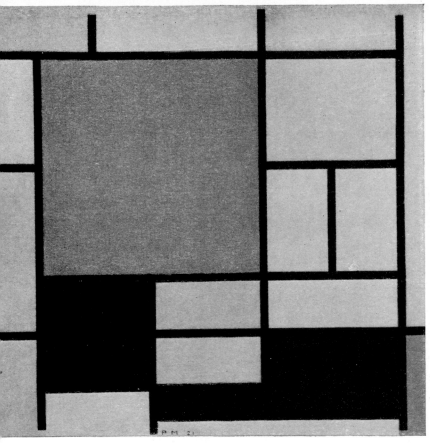

Piet Mondrian *Composition with Red, Yellow, Blue and Black* 1921
Oil. Collection Haags Gemeentemuseum, The Hague

4 De Stijl: achievements

Van Doesburg's adoption of the diagonal element in his paintings
was one of the reasons that led Mondrian to disassociate himself
finally from De Stijl in 1925. (He also disliked van Doesburg's support for the Dadaists.) This probably provided a convenient excuse
as Mondrian was reclusive by nature, and having found his way intended to pursue it single-mindedly without reference to what

95

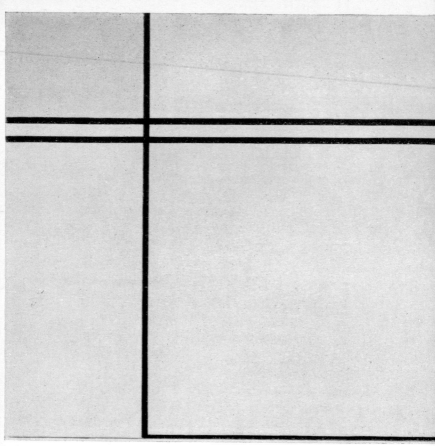

Piet Mondrian *Composition* 1932
Oil. Courtesy Marlborough Gallery, London

other artists were doing. Mondrian's work had evolved into what
was to be his mature style in the compositions of 1921 with their
rectangular flat planes of primary colour bound by black lines
which often stop slightly short of the edge of the painting. These
works are marked by a strong asymmetry of composition yet retain
the balance that Mondrian regarded as so important. Through the
'twenties and 'thirties his work becomes progressively refined and
dematerialized.

Piet Mondrian *Lozenge with Grey Lines* 1918
Oil. Mondrian did use diagonals at this time.
Collection Haags Gemeentemuseum, The Hague

In Mondrian's paintings of 1921 one can see the beginning of a development away from the emphasis on the central parts of the composition towards an emphasis on the extreme periphery which becomes even more marked in his works of the late 'twenties. One gets the impression that the painting continues unseen beyond the limits of the edge of the canvas. In his counter-compositions van Doesburg succeeds in achieving a similar effect with more dynamic means.

Theo van Doesburg *Counter-construction* 1923
Gouache. Collection Mrs N. van Doesburg

98

Theo van Doesburg, *Counter-composition* 1924
Gouache. Collection Centraal Museum, Utrecht

By the mid-'twenties van Doesburg was no longer interested in preserving balance and equilibrium. In 1926 he wrote in *De Stijl*: 'In counter-composition, equilibrium in the plane plays a less important part. Each plane is part of peripheric space and construction has to be more conceived as a phenomenon of tension than as one of relations in the plane.'

In Rietveld's red-blue chair, the black horizontal members provide the structural frame of the chair, the support. The two diagonal boards transfer the weight of the sitter to this frame and, when the chair is empty, seem visually to represent symbolically or abstractly the sitter, the human figure. This diagonal abstraction of the human figure re-enters De Stijl in van Doesburg's counter-compositions, but unlike Rietveld's chair it is not held in balance, it is dynamic.

Theo van Doesburg *Counter-composition V* 1924
Oil. Collection Stedelijk Museum, Amsterdam

100

Theo van Doesburg and **Cornelis van Eesteren** Design for Amsterdam university hall, 1923

Van Doesburg wrote about his similar use of the dynamic diagonal in the decoration of the Aubette in these terms in 1928: 'The track of man in space (from the left to the right, from front to back, from above to below) has become of fundamental importance for painting in architecture.'

Van Doesburg's first use of the dynamic diagonal seems to have been in a scheme for the hall of Amsterdam university, designed in collaboration with van Eesteren. Maybe the idea of using diagonals came originally from the diagonal lines (indicating three-dimensional relationships) in architects' isometric drawings, such as those produced in 1923, when van Doesburg also collaborated with van Eesteren on the design for a private house commissioned by Léonce Rosenberg in Paris and a projected 'house for an artist'.

The university hall (like the two houses) was never built, which is a tragedy, because from the drawings it appears to have been at least as exciting a design as the Aubette. Some of the exhilaration that must have been felt in the cinema-café room of the Aubette can be seen in van Doesburg's *Counter-composition*, in the Gemeente-museum, the Hague (page 8). For the dance-hall of the Aubette, van Doesburg used only horizontal and vertical planes

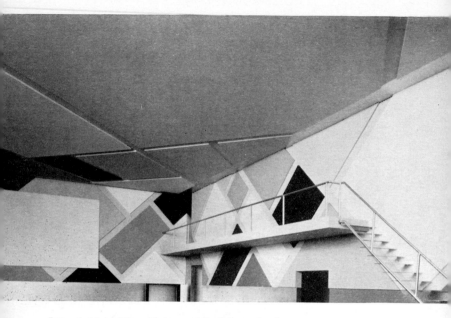

Reconstruction of the café-cinema of the Aubette, Strasbourg,
1927, designed by **Theo van Doesburg** (original destroyed)
Collection Stedelijk van Abbemuseum Eindhoven

on pages 102 *and* 103 Reconstruction of the dance-hall of the
Aubette, Strasbourg, 1927, designed by **Theo van Doesburg** (original
destroyed)
Collection Stedelijk van Abbemuseum, Eindhoven

Theo van Doesburg Café-cinema, Aubette, Strasbourg, 1927 (destroyed)

and lines, presumably because there was sufficient 'movement' in the art of dancing itself. For the sedentary café-cinema van Doesburg used the more dynamic diagonal schemes. The café-cinema was decorated in two shades of red, two yellows, green, blue, black, white and two shades of grey, the dance-hall with the same colours, except that blue and green are replaced by two shades of blue. One of the most dramatic features of the dance-hall was the grouping of light bulbs in rows to make up square panels of points of light on ceiling and walls.

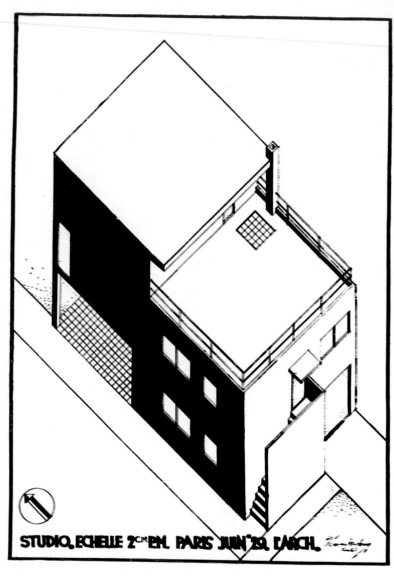

STUDIO, ECHELLE 2ᶜᴹ P.M. PARIS JUIN 29. L'ARCH.

Theo van Doesburg and **Cornelis van Eesteren** Design for van Doesburg's studio at Meudon, near Paris, 1929
From *De Stijl* 1932 (last, memorial number)

Theo van Doesburg and **Cornelis van Eesteren** Studio for van Doesburg
Photograph from *De Stijl* 1932 (last, memorial number)

Van Doesburg's last important work was his design for his own studio at Meudon, near Paris, for which he also designed the furniture and fitments. Suitably for a private home and work-place (rather than a public or social centre like the café-cinema of the Aubette or the university hall), van Doesburg composed his studio in restful horizontals. It is a design of quiet subtlety and balanced purity. Van Doesburg had intended it to be the centre of renewed De Stijl activity as well as his studio, but he died before it was finished. He was forty-seven.

Theo van Doesburg and **Cornelis van Eesteren** Design for house,
commissioned by Léonce Rosenberg, 1923 (not executed)

It might be said of van Doesburg as has been said by Maxwell
Fry of Moholy-Nagy, that the trouble was that he always had
six ideas at once. Having found an idea van Doesburg would
sometimes only hastily sketch it out before rushing onto the next
idea. He had tremendous energy and enthusiasm and the capacity
to inspire others, although sometimes this was taken to the point
of aggression and he would turn his former collaborators against
108

Theo van Doesburg and **Cornelis van Eesteren** Model of house for an artist, 1923 (not executed)

him. Van Doesburg left relatively few paintings and the quality of these is uneven. Yet he was an important painter and could have been a great one if he had wanted to. After 1920 he became less and less interested in being a painter of finished easel pictures. Most of his paintings are not particularly well-finished; even before he began to collaborate on a large scale with architects his paintings look like sketches for environmental works.

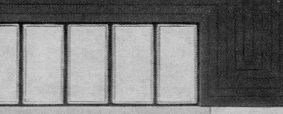

CAFE · RESTAURANT

CAFE DE UNIE CAFE

DE · UNIE

Theo van Doesburg *Composition 17* 1919
Oil. Collection Haags Gemeentemuseum, The Hague

J.J.P.Oud Coloured drawing for the Café Unie, Rotterdam, 1925
Collection Mrs J.M.A.Oud-Dinaux

Photograph of a room at the van Doesburg exhibition at the Stedelijk van
Abbemuseum, Eindhoven 1968/69, showing the tubular furniture designed
by van Doesburg for his studio at Meudon, 1929. The stained glass on the left
was designed by van Doesburg in 1921

John Berger has recently written, in a review of a book by Max Raphael (a critic cited by van Doesburg in his Bauhaus book) that: 'Since 1848 every artist unready to be a mere paid entertainer has tried to resist the bourgeoisation of his finished work, the transformation of the spiritual value of his work into property value.'

This is particularly true of van Doesburg. Like Moholy-Nagy and Lissitzky, van Doesburg was not a great artist in terms of a large body of major paintings. Like them he was one of the great catalyst figures of the 'twenties and like them his work has to be judged as a whole, as painter, writer, typographer, designer and propagandist. Taken in this way their contribution to twentieth-century art is as important as that of the great innovators like Kandinsky, Mondrian and Malevich.

The relationship of van Doesburg's work to that of Mondrian is similar to that of Lissitzky or Moholy-Nagy to Malevich. They saw the implications of the experiments in pure painting of Mondrian and Malevich in terms of typographical, architectural and environmental developments as much as in painting and were able to lay the foundations for these in their own works and in their writings. Their aim was to bring art closer to life.

Rietveld's most important early commission was the interior with furniture and fittings for Dr Hartog at Maarsen. This has been destroyed and all that remains is a few photographs which nonetheless show the character of this extraordinary work. The rectilinearity of the furniture is relieved by a circle painted on the wall. The chest of shallow drawers is an obvious relative of the buffet (page 26) with its protruding structural members and gaps between each drawer so that each remains visually discrete. The light-fitting is one of the simplest and most effective of all Rietveld's designs. The four long bulbs were standard Philips' fitments. Rietveld attached black-painted wooden cubes to either end and suspended them from the ceiling with flex, two horizontally and two vertically. Another version with only one vertical element was made for the Schröder house.

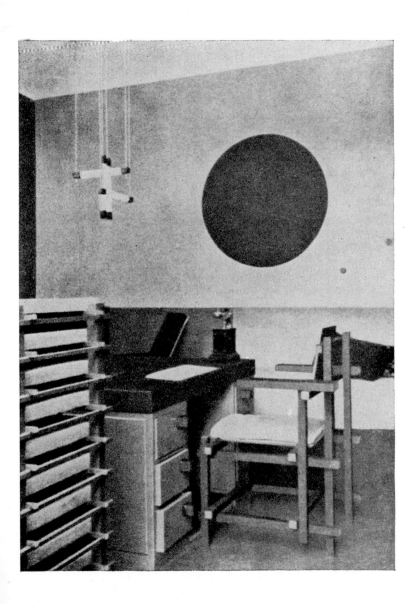

Gerrit Rietveld Interior for Dr Hartog, Maarsen, 1920 (destroyed)

115

Gerrit Rietveld Hanging lamp, 1920

Gerrit Rietveld *Construction c.* 1920
Collection Centraal Museum, Utrecht

The light-fittings that Rietveld designed for the interior of a jewellery shop in Amsterdam about the same time consisted simply of clusters of bare bulbs suspended at different distances from the ceiling. Rietveld also used this system of hanging bare bulbs in the remodelling of an interior in 1921 for Mrs Schröder, for whom he later designed the Schröder house. A small lamp that Rietveld designed in 1925 consisted principally of a single bare bulb painted black except for a small circular area at the bottom (see page 118).

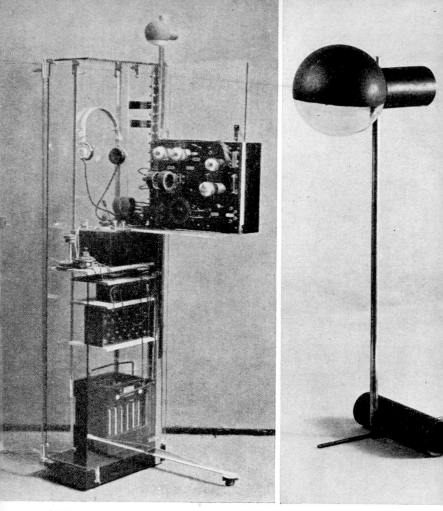

Gerrit Rietveld with **T. Schröder-Schräder** Radio cabinet 1925 (destroyed) Designed to show all the functioning parts of the radio equipment. The lamp at the top is similar to Rietveld's table lamp (see right). Unfortunately when completed the radio did not work. The mechanic who was called in loosened the wrong screw and the glass cabinet was shattered. It was never repaired.

The Schröder house was the first complete building designed by Rietveld. He had originally been a cabinet-maker, following his father's trade, but had studied architecture at night school under Klaarhamer. The site for the Schröder house was picked because it was the only one available with access to the country. When

Gerrit Rietveld Schröder house, Prins Hendriklaan, Utrecht, 1924

it was built it was the last house in the town, looking across meadows. Unfortunately the site has now been disfigured by a raised motorway, although even this visual and auditory intrusion cannot destroy the relationship that the house creates between the space within it and the space outside.

It has often been claimed that van Doesburg and van Eesteren's plan for a house for Léonce Rosenberg of 1923 (for which Rietveld made a model) influenced his design of the Schröder house.

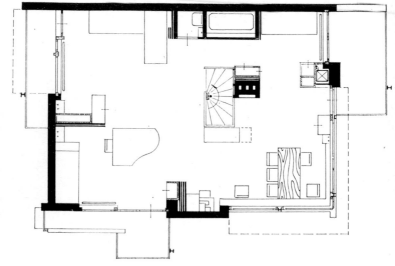

Schröder house plan, first floor (open)

This is probably true, although Rietveld's design is far more radical than even his own cardboard model for the 1923 scheme which is still basically a series of cubic volumes, loosely held together, although some of van Doesburg's drawings related to this scheme are closer to the Schröder house. The more direct parallel is with Rietveld's own chair made for an exhibition in Berlin in 1923, an asymmetrical composition of planes only. There is no framework of wooden rails as with the red-blue chair and most of Rietveld's other early chairs (see page 126).

That Rietveld succeeded in achieving what van Doesburg and van Eesteren had envisaged in their schemes is clear from van Doesburg's immediate enthusiasm for the Schröder house. It remains the only realization in terms of actual architecture of the most advanced spatial ideas of De Stijl.

The planes that form its walls and windows, balconies and roof seem to fly out into space in an even more daring and exhilarating way than the wooden rails of the red-blue chair, although directly related to it. On the first floor the windows swing open so that the space inside the house flows through into the garden. The space

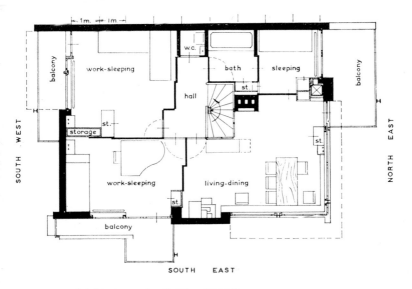

Schröder house plan, first floor (closed)

outside flows into the interior. The apple trees in the garden appear to live inside the house with its occupants. The partitions which divide the upper floor can be slid right back so that the whole floor becomes an envelope of space where only the arrangement of the furniture and the activity of the inhabitants defines the function of any particular area. Alternatively, the partitions can be closed if privacy is desired, forming four separate rooms. It is the first modern open-plan house; the first truly flexible dwelling which takes into account the increasing informality and freedom of social and living arrangements in the twentieth century.

Rietveld was never a functionalist. He was too far ahead of his time for that. He realized that the functions of a modern building are liable to change continually. Here he was probably helped by the far-sightedness of his patron Truus Schröder-Schräder who acted as a collaborator with Rietveld on the design of the interior of her house and also on some later schemes. She insisted that each room (or partitionable space on the upper floor) should be equipped with a bed, cooking facilities and a sink. Many years later, during the Second World War, Mrs Schröder had to let off

several rooms in the house, and the fittings in each room proved to have been a very practical forethought. Throughout the forty-five years of its existence the interior arrangements have been constantly changed around. Until his death in 1964, Rietveld added new furniture and fitments to Mrs Schröder's requirements, such as the elegant metal staircase leading up to the skylight. Originally the kitchen was on the ground floor and there was a room for a servant behind. Now there is no servant the kitchen has been moved upstairs. The Schröder house was planned with the living area upstairs while downstairs are small enclosed rooms for studying and other private activities. (Le Corbusier was similarly to plan the living areas on the first floor of the Villa Savoie—designed five years after the Schröder house.) When Mrs Schröder's children were

Interior of Schröder house, summer 1968, showing some later additions (by Rietveld) like the metal staircase. Zig-zag chair designed by Rietveld in 1934. Detail (left) hanging lamp (1920) and partition round stair-well, metal staircase beyond.
Photographs, the author

Gerrit Rietveld Schröder House, from the back, showing the corner which 'disappears' when the windows are opened
Photograph, Brian Housden

growing up the first floor was often partitioned off to give them the privacy they needed. When they left home it became open again; it can be opened during the day and closed at night. The changes the house has undergone since it was built is the record of the life and changing circumstances of a family. Its admirable flexibility enabled the house to be easily adapted to suit the occupants' changing needs.

In 1928 Rietveld wrote: 'Functional architecture must not just slavishly satisfy existing needs; it must also reveal living conditions.'

Although many commentators, including Walter Gropius, have assumed that the Schröder house is constructed of reinforced concrete this is not so. Only the foundations and the balcony slabs are of concrete. The rest of the house is traditional Dutch brick and wood construction, although steel I-beams are used for lintels and to support the roof and balconies. At the time when it was built, reinforced concrete would have been beyond the modest budget allowed for the house. Also it was the first complete building that Rietveld had designed and he was possibly chary of using this new method of construction. The steel I-beams above the windows are painted black so that they disappear in the shadow of the roof and balcony planes; the brick is rendered over and painted white and grey to look like concrete. It is unlikely that Rietveld intended to deliberately deceive anyone. His house is a statement of what *could* be done in concrete (and many architects since have taken Rietveld's point), just as the red-blue chair was a statement of what *could* be done in terms of mass-production or standardization. (No manufacturer ever gave Rietveld the chance to realize this himself.)

The Schröder house looks tenuously balanced, like a pack of cards. So much so that apparently crowds gathered round it, shortly after it was completed, waiting for its imminent collapse! In the Fagus factory (see page 22) Gropius had moved the corner supports back so that the glass met, separated by only a thin metal corner-piece. In the east corner on the upper floor of the Schröder house Rietveld produced an even more visually exciting solution. The steel structural beam supporting the roof is moved about a foot to one side. A long window on the south-east side and a small window on the north-east meet at the east corner where this

Gerrit Rietveld Berlin Chair, 1923
The chair was exhibited in Berlin in an interior by Huszar. Collection Mr and
Mrs Brian Housden

structural support has been displaced. When these two windows
are opened the corner disappears. The wide-flung windows extend
into the space around the house like the wooden rails of the
red-blue chair and seem to direct and channel the flow of outside
space into the interior.

Rietveld believed that architecture (or furniture) by limiting
space, made space 'real', that space doesn't exist until it is
limited. Similarly, objects and materials only become real or visible
through their limitation.

Standing before a Rietveld chair or sitting in one, you are made
acutely conscious of the relationship of your own body to the
things around you and to the space that your own body occupies.
In the Schröder house one is exhilaratingly aware of space as an
almost tangible entity.

Many years after designing the Schröder house Rietveld wrote:
'If, for a particular purpose, we separate, limit and bring into a
human scale a part of unlimited space, it is (if all goes well) a piece
of space brought to life as reality. In this way, a special segment of
space has been absorbed into our human system.' (1957)

Georges Vantongerloo *Groupe y = ax² bx + c* 1931
Wood painted grey. Courtesy Marlborough Gallery, London

It is fairly clear that Rietveld regarded his furniture as much as a kind of sculpture as furniture, and his earlier pieces produced in the years immediately before and after 1920 offer visual parallels with the sculpture of Vantongerloo, whose view of space was close to that of Rietveld, although expressed usually in more philosophical, less pragmatic terms:

Since man moves, the concept of space is inherent in him. Our senses imply the notion. Without our senses, it is obvious that we should not need it. We need space in order to situate objects. Space, which is indispensable to us (though we cannot define it), is inseparable from life. We cannot conceive of existence without space. (1930)

In Vantongerloo's sculpture of the late 'twenties and early 'thirties volume is replaced by planes or elements similar to those of Rietveld's early furniture. The positive-negative, volume-void interchange is replaced by a definition and extension of space by means of planes or elements. These fly out and seemingly hover in space with the same quality of exhilaration as the elements of

127

Rietveld's buffet, the planes of the Berlin chair or the walls, balconies and open windows of the Schröder house.

Rietveld's early chairs measure out space with their discrete, visually separated elements. But the space that they measure out is our own space, because as well as being a kind of sculpture these are chairs whose scale is directly related to the human body they are designed to accommodate. As we look at them they are a kind of abstraction of our own bodies sitting in space. When we sit in them we are made aware of our own body and its relationship to and displacement of space by the pressure of the hard wood on our limbs.

Nikolaus Pevsner has called the red-blue armchair (in *Sources of Modern Architecture and Design*) : 'the first piece of furniture embodying the principles of De Stijl—where comfort has yielded to geometry.' In fact the red-blue chair is reasonably comfortable, although it does tend to *look* uncomfortable. There is an early photograph of Rietveld sitting in the first version of the chair (it had side-pieces) about 1918, surrounded by his grinning carpenters. He looks perfectly at ease and comfortable ; nor does his pose look feigned. In the early version the red-blue chair does not seem to have been red, blue, black and yellow at all. It appears to have been unpainted and in this state it was illustrated in 1919 in the *De Stijl* magazine. Presumably it was painted later on, perhaps at the suggestion of van Doesburg.

The colour makes it look more uncomfortable than it is. The red plank of the back coming forward, the blue plane of the seat receding. You perhaps subconsciously feel that the back will slap you and the seat disappear under you. However, although the colour may make the chair look more uncomfortable it undoubtedly adds to its effect as sculpture, dematerializing the planes, making the seat and back appear to float on air, because the black-painted frame tends to disappear visually (particularly on a dark floor or against dark walls, as was intended).

One of the functions of Rietveld's chairs, with their hard seats and backs, is to focus our senses, to make us alert and aware. Rietveld was not interested in conventional ideas of comfort (the nineteenth-century armchair that relaxes you so much that you spill your coffee or fall asleep over your book). He wished to keep the sitter physically and mentally 'toned up'.

Rietveld sitting in the first version of the red-blue chair surrounded by his carpenters (about 1919)

Mrs Schröder has written of this chair:

But a chair being a piece of furniture has still other functions than being or looking comfortable or 'not uncomfortable'. It should, like the other furniture, help to realize the space of a room, to make of interior space: interior architecture—developing and enriching the sensory perceptions of space, colour etc. It should . . . not disturb space working (as it most of the time does, if you do not pay attention) but it should let space pass through and around —realizing each other. If you translate 'to sit' into Dutch it is *Zitten* and Zitten is also an activity. (From a letter to the author)

Gerrit Rietveld Row-houses, Utrecht; left 1930–31, right 1934

Gerrit Rietveld Shop, Zaudy, Wesel (Germany), 1928 (destroyed)

In the 'twenties Rietveld had mainly worked on private commissions for remodelling interiors or on the alteration of shop-fronts, some of which were among his most exciting works, like Zaudy at Wesel, in Germany. In the 'thirties Rietveld produced some interesting experiments in low-cost housing, although mainly designed for the middle classes rather than the working class, like Oud's housing schemes. In the late 'twenties Rietveld experimented with some revolutionary ideas that unfortunately he was never given the chance to develop further. These were the use of

130

Gerrit Rietveld Chauffeur's house and garage, Utrecht, 1927–28

Gerrit Rietveld Crate furniture (chair) 1934
Collection Stedelijk Museum, Amsterdam

prefabricated concrete planks, one metre by three, on a framework of steel I-beams, in the chauffeur's house of 1927–28, and his scheme of 1929 (exhibited but never executed) of the 'core house', the central services area of which (stairs, hall, bathroom, piping, wiring, etc) were to be made in a factory and the rest of the house built round it *in situ* according to the number of rooms needed, etc. In 1934 he designed 'crate furniture' which could be assembled by the purchaser from pre-cut boxwood parts. This seems to have been one of the earliest examples of inexpensive knock-down furniture.

Gerrit Rietveld Crate furniture (table) 1934
Collection Stedelijk Museum, Amsterdam

Oud's Café Unie (see page 15), destroyed in the bombing of Rotterdam in 1940, looks closer to Mondrian's compositions of the early 'twenties than to Rietveld's chair or the Schröder house. This might seem to confirm the argument of van Doesburg and Oud that painting influenced architecture at this time. However, the

J.J.P.Oud Temporary manager's hut for the Oud-Mathenesse housing estate, 1923
The hut was painted in primary colours

J.J.P.Oud Photograph taken in the 'thirties by Moholy-Nagy

parallel with van Doesburg's layout of the cover of the *De Stijl* magazine from 1921 is even closer.

The photographs of the street frontage reveal it to have been an essentially two-dimensional façade. Architecture is basically three-dimensional, concerned with space we can move about in. But it can sometimes have other functions. The front of a shop or a restaurant is a sign beckoning the passer-by. Oud brilliantly incorporates lettering as part of the façade, relating it to the solid and transparent elements (windows and walling), drawing the passer-by's attention to the kind of building it is, leading the eye down to its ground-floor windows through which the interior of the café can be seen and to the door through which he is invited to enter. Here the New Typography is ingeniously combined to serve a practical purpose (advertisement) and also to contribute an exciting and exhilarating element to the urban landscape. This has now become commonplace, but never quite so subtly and imaginatively realized as in Oud's Unie.

Like the Café Unie, the temporary manager's hut for the Oud-Matthenesse (*oud* means 'old' in Dutch) is one of Oud's most remarkable and imaginative works. Although great attention is given to the surface of the walling, with its quasi-concentric geometric motif (used also in the Unie), this small building is an exception

135

J.J.P.Oud Housing estate at Hook of Holland, designed 1924
136

among Oud's work in that it is as much a spatial as a surface composition, albeit of spatial volume, rather than of planes, as in Rietveld's Schröder house. Oud's best work always has an exceptional purity, none more than this little shed. The way in which the series of windows which give top-lighting are visually separated from the roof by only the thinnest of lines is highly refined, and the handling of surfaces and inter-relation of volumes is of extreme sensitivity.

The Oud-Matthenesse estate itself was more conventional than the temporary manager's hut, in the tradition of Dutch single-storey cottages with sharply pitched roofs. In the detailing of the façades, chimneys and lintels however, Oud's refinement of design is clearly revealed.

These commissions were undertaken after he had severed his connection with De Stijl. As early as the first volume of the magazine Oud had written:

The subordination of the utilitarian to the idealistic aspect would be detrimental to the cultural and general values and would only hamper the striving for style. For the development of an architectural style, a good house (in the sense of technical and practical purity) is therefore of greater importance than a beautiful house.

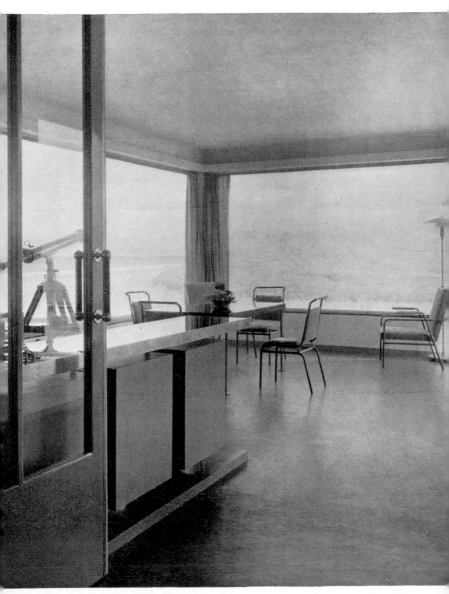

In his Hook and Kiefhoek schemes Oud achieved an architectural style in which a good house was also a beautiful house. Oud wrote of 'the need for number and measure, for cleanliness and order, for standardization and repetition, for perfection and high finish'. He created a style that was anonymous but not inhuman, comparable in this way to the anonymous domestic architecture of Holland in the seventeenth century and of France and England in the eighteenth century. These housing schemes are among the earliest examples of the International Style so widely adopted since and so often debased.

The Hook of Holland estate is quite different from Oud-Matthenesse. Instead of separate cottages the terraces of houses are integrated together into long streamlined blocks with rounded corners and balconies which extend the full length of the terraces. The extent of each living unit is defined by the dividing metal fences at balcony level and the low-walled areas in front of the front doors. The curved end of the terraces form shops and the curve of the glass shop-fronts and concrete cantilevered slabs which offer protection to the shopper from rain or sun, provide focal points and an element of visual drama. The smooth white surface of the façades is contrasted with the rough texture of the cobbles and sets of road and pavement.

J.J.P.Oud Housing estate at Hook of Holland, designed 1924
Rounded shop-fronts

J.J.P.Oud Kiefhoek housing estate, Rotterdam, 1925–9

In Kiefhoek, designed in the following year, the rounded shop ends are more restrained, the protective concrete canopy less dramatic, but the treatment of the terraces is more sophisticated. The windows form a continuous band and each separate house is not so deliberately divided from its neighbour as at Hook. Yet visiting Kiefhoek today, beautifully kept, with the window of each front

J.J.P.Oud Kiefhoek housing estate, Rotterdam, 1925–9

on pages 144 *and* 145
J.J.P.Oud Drawing for housing scheme, Blijdorp, Rotterdam, 1931 (not executed)

room containing a different arrangement of potted plants, you never feel that the individual household is submerged completely in the social ideal. The idea of an urban village which makes no concessions to cottaginess seems to work well. Nothing so successful seems to have been achieved in the rebuilding of Rotterdam since the last war. The contrast between the cobbled

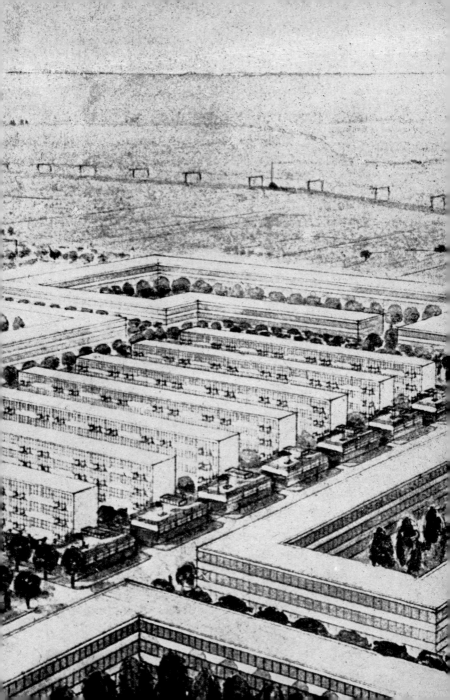

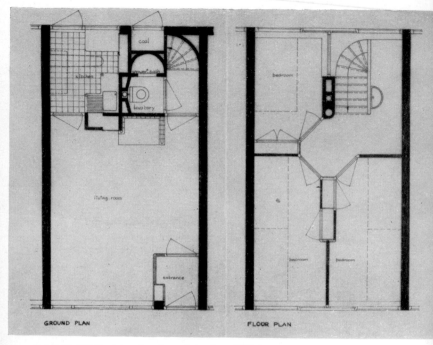

GROUND PLAN

FLOOR PLAN

J.J.P.Oud Kiefhoek housing estate, Rotterdam, 1925–9
Ground and first floor plan of terrace houses

road and the smooth façades is repeated, as at Hook, and there is
more use of exposed brick in the garden walls and beneath the
lower windows. The lintels and window-frames are gaily painted
in bright colours. In Oud's Kiefhoek, as with the Schröder house,
one feels a realization of the balance between the private and the
social, the individual and the universal, which was the most important principle of De Stijl.

146

J.J.P.Oud Drawing for housing scheme, Blijdorp, Rotterdam, 1931 (not executed)

5 Conclusions

Van Doesburg embraced Dadaism because he saw that the De Stijl belief that art must be extended into life itself (and perhaps consequently disappear as a separate entity) and the Dadaist attack on art and society brought artists to the same point although from two different directions. It would seem that of the three great catalyst figures of the 'twenties (Moholy-Nagy, Lissitzky, van Doesburg) van Doesburg was the first to realize this. Moholy-Nagy has described what happened at the Constructivist-Dadaist congress in 1922:

The Constructivists living in Germany . . . called a congress in October of 1922, in Weimar. Arriving there, to our great amazement we found also the Dadaists, Hans Arp and Tristan Tzara. This caused a rebellion against the host, Doesburg, because at that time we felt in Dadaism a destructive and obsolete force in comparison with the new outlook of the Constructivists.

Doesburg, a powerful personality, quieted the storm and the guests were accepted to the dismay of the younger, purist members who slowly withdrew and let the congress turn into a Dadaistic performance. At that time, we did not realize that Doesburg himself was both a Constructivist and Dadaist, writing Dada poems under the pen name of I.K.Bonset.

(*Vision in Motion*, Chicago 1947)

In 1922–23 van Doesburg edited four issues of a Dadaist magazine *Mecano* which he published from Leiden (running concurrently with *De Stijl*). In 1921 he had written to Kok: 'I intend to edit a splendid bulletin, on the meanest paper existing, but still very modern.' The four issues appeared on yellow, blue, red and white paper respectively. The first three issues were printed on both sides of a large folded broadsheet, the last issue on four similar sheets. In the last (white) issue van Doesburg wrote an article entitled 'Towards a Constructive Poetry' in which he refers to 'the blue-jackets of the new Constructivist art' and writes: 'To accept the purely utilitarian as the whole foundation for a new art form = madness.'

(Uit de serie: SOLDATEN 1916)

RUITER

Stap
Paard
STAP
PAARD
Stap
Paard.

STAPPE   PAARD
STAPPE   PAARD
STAPPE   PAARD
STAPPE PAARD STAPPE PAARD
STEPPE PAARD STEPPE PAARD
STEPPE PAARD STEPPE PAARD
STIPPE PAARD STIPPE PAARD STIPPE PAARD

STIP   PAARD
STIP   PAARD
STIP

WOLK

162

VOORBIJTREKKENDE TROEP

Ran   sel
Ran   sel
Ran   sel
Ran-sel
Ran-sel
Ran-sel
Ran-sel
Ran-sel

BLik - ken - tr**o**mmel
BLik - ken - tr**o**mmel

BLikken TRommel

RANSEL

BLikken trommel

BLikken trommel

BLikken trommel

RANSEL

I.K.Bonset (Theo van Doesburg) Poems from *De Stijl*, 1921

Hans Richter has described a Dadaist lecture tour of Holland that van Doesburg made with his wife and Kurt Schwitters:

After Does had once experienced Dada, he threw himself into it wholeheartedly. With his wife—the pianist Nelly van Doesburg, who played modern music—and with Schwitters, he executed a unique Dada tour of Holland, in which Does appeared as orator and expounded the Spirit of Dada. In these expositions, he was interrupted from time to time by a member of the audience who gave a very realistic imitation of a barking dog. When the audience made ready to eject the enormously tall gentleman who was doing the barking, the speaker on the platform introduced him as Kurt Schwitters. (Hans Richter, *Dadaism*, London 1965)

Rietveld Chair, 1919
This replica made under the direction of Rietveld is in a different wood from the original which was exhibited at the Bauhaus in 1923. Collection Mr & Mrs Brian Housden

Richter also describes van Doesburg's collaboration with Arp and his wife, Sophie Taüber-Arp, on the Aubette:

Each of the three decorated one-third of the building. In this way they produced the first great abstract frescoes. Arp's agile arabesques, Doesburg's Neo-plastic purism and Sophie's lively divisions of space did not conflict with each other. They complemented each other. Anti-art and art had come together, and now each gazed into the other's face as if in a mirror, restored to youth and, as if miraculously, sprung from the same stock.

Prophetically van Doesburg realized that a purely utilitarian Constructivism would produce stony fruit. The only true way forward was by a synthesis of the mainstream tradition of twentieth-century art and design (De Stijl, Constructivism) with the 'other tradition' of Dadaism.

The relationship between De Stijl and the Bauhaus is interesting although confused. From Holland, van Doesburg had been an early admirer of the Bauhaus, but when he visited it at Weimar early in 1921 he was bitterly disappointed.

It has been said that van Doesburg had earlier been promised a job at the Bauhaus and that when he arrived at Weimar Gropius went back on his word. Gropius has denied this, saying that van Doesburg only asked him for a job when he arrived in 1921. (It is not denied that van Doesburg was refused the post.) Whatever the truth of the matter, van Doesburg's subsequent attacks on the Bauhaus are unlikely to have been the result of personal spite. From all accounts, the Bauhaus was in a period of crisis at that time and full of contradictions. In *De Stijl* in 1922 van Doesburg wrote that the Bauhaus was as much a parody of modern ideas as the church was a parody of Christianity and described the Expressionist-orientated designs being produced there as 'ultra-baroque'. As he had not been given a teaching post at the Bauhaus, van Doesburg started his own Stijl course in Weimar in 1922. This was attended by many Bauhaus students, particularly those who disliked Itten's Expressionist and self-expressionist influence. Van Doesburg's aggressive lectures (he lampooned the arty-crafty cradle that the students had designed for Itten's new-born baby, for instance) served to focus the unrest that was already fermenting under the surface among many of the Bauhaus students. Van Doesburg did not, as he later claimed, single-handedly alter the direction of the Bauhaus, but he was a powerful influence in bringing the crisis of 1921–22 to a head. The change came when Itten resigned and Gropius appointed Moholy-Nagy in his place.

In 1923 Gropius invited Rietveld to contribute to an exhibition to be shown during the Bauhaus week. Rietveld sent a chair of 1919 (see page 150). Van Doesburg was furious at this collaboration with the enemy and wrote an angry letter to Rietveld which is quoted by Theodore Brown in his monograph on Rietveld. The postcript read : 'I have given up completely the desire to work towards a collective goal. I am very sad because of this kick from *you*, from whom I *least* expected it.'

By 1924 van Doesburg, however, was reconciled to the Bauhaus, probably as a result of the changes that had been made there. At any rate relations were sufficiently cordial for van Doesburg's *Principles of Neo-Plastic Art* to appear in the series of Bauhaus Books in 1925. (Mondrian's essays on Neo-plasticism and Oud's essays on Dutch architecture were also published as Bauhaus Books.)

In 1923 Léonce Rosenberg invited van Doesburg to show the architectural ideas of De Stijl at his Paris gallery *L'Effort Moderne*. The exhibition included the model and drawings for a private house that Rosenberg had commissioned, the designs for an artist's house and for the hall of a university, all by van Doesburg and van Eesteren. There were also drawings and photographs of work by the other architects and designers who had been associated with De Stijl.

This exhibition was so successful that a further show was organized in Paris at the *Ecole Spéciale d'Architecture* in 1924 and later the same year the exhibition moved to Nancy in eastern France. No doubt these two exhibitions stimulated French architects and designers. Le Corbusier's use of colour in interiors seems to date from about this time.

In 1925 De Stijl was excluded from the *Arts Décoratifs* exhibition in Paris. Van Doesburg was furious that the Dutch authorities had not invited the De Stijl designers to participate. De Stijl principles were, however, displayed in the Austrian pavilion, designed by Frederic Kiesler, who had been associated with De Stijl since 1923. With the Schröder house this was the most daring and imaginative spatial conception of De Stijl actually executed. A counter-exhibition was organized for work which had been refused, entitled *L'Art d'Aujourd'hui*, which included a comprehensive display of recent De Stijl work.

Frederik Kiesler 'City in Space'
Shown in the Austrian Pavilion, Exposition des Arts Decoratifs, Paris 1925

Van Doesburg's *The Cow*, 1917 compared with **Gropius'** director's house,
Bauhaus, Dessau, 1926 (*opposite*)
From *De Stijl* by Alfred H. Barr, Museum of Modern Art, New York, 1961

Many attempts have been made to show the influence of De
Stijl painting—as opposed to De Stijl architecture and design—on
the architecture and design of the 'twenties, both at the Bauhaus
and elsewhere. Not many of these attempts are very convincing.
One of the more plausible is Alfred H. Barr's juxtaposition of Gropius' director's house for the Dessau Bauhaus (1926) with van
Doesburg's painting *The Cow* (1916–17). The visual parallel is
154

certainly compelling. However, there are many earlier architectural precedents for Gropius' use of asymmetrically arranged elements; for instance, the Californian architect Irving Gill's Walter Dodge house, Los Angeles (1915–16), or, much earlier, Godwin's white house designed for Whistler. However, it is amusing to believe that one of the most important elements in modern architecture, asymmetricality, might be derived from a Dutch cow!

The works of van Doesburg that were certainly influential on the subsequent development of modern architecture are his drawings and plans for the house for Léonce Rosenberg of 1923 and for the 'artist's house' (with van Eesteren). Van Eesteren's own important influence on the development of town-planning is undoubted. (He was appointed chief civil engineer/town planner for Amsterdam in 1929.)

The one specific area where De Stijl influence on the Bauhaus seems certain is in furniture design. A film strip made of the development of Marcel Breuer's furniture shows the direct impingement of Rietveld's chair shown at the Bauhaus Week exhibition, although in his 1924 wooden chair Breuer has already developed the idea in the direction of greater flexibility (as Rietveld himself had done since making the 1919 chair, in two leather-seated chairs). Breuer's first tubular chair, the 'Wassily' chair, is an ingenious combination of elements derived from Thonet and Rietveld. The curious side-pieces of canvas under the arm-pieces, for instance, must come from the wooden side-pieces in Rietveld's 1919 chair, or from the first version of the red-blue armchair as illustrated in *De Stijl* in 1919.

Film strip showing development of furniture designed by
Marcel Breuer at the Bauhaus

Rudolf Schindler's Lovell beach house at Newport Beach, California, has sometimes been compared with Rietveld's Schröder house. In fact Schindler's house is closer to the van Doesburg–van Eesteren projects exhibited in Paris in 1923 with its long horizontals of the balconies, assembling space in terms of loosely enclosed volumes rather than of intersecting planes. Certainly it merits comparison with the Schröder house, but when one considers that it was designed as a beach house in an ideally warm climate, its penetration of the interior by 'outside' spaces seems less extraordinary in this context than Rietveld's house which was designed to be lived in all the time and to accommodate all the changing needs of a family.

Whether Schindler was influenced by De Stijl is difficult to say. Reyner Banham's argument that 'European architectural publications just didn't reach California in those days (survivors of the 'twenties can testify to this)' isn't very convincing. Schindler trained as an architect in the Vienna of Loos, Wagner and Hoffmann, the Vienna that was the first to appreciate Mackintosh. After he had gone to America (first to Chicago and then California) he kept himself well-informed of what was going on in Europe. Apparently sketches for the Lovell beach house have been found dating back to 1923, which would accord with the house being closer to the van Doesburg-van Eesteren projects. Although these were not illustrated until 1924 in the *De Stijl* magazine they were probably reproduced in reports of the 1923 Paris exhibition. On the other hand with his Austrian background and the example of Wright (for whom Schindler worked in Chicago) and of Californian architects like Irving Gill, he could have arrived at a similar point with his beach house quite independently.

One should not take the statements of artists and architects too literally. Although there is considerable stylistic unity in the work of those artists associated with De Stijl there was also diversity and strong individuality. The Bauhaus claimed to be an idea, not a style, but nevertheless imposed a style on its designers, if not on the painters. Both De Stijl and the Bauhaus must share some of

Rudolf Schindler Lovell beach house, Newport Beach,
California, 1925–6

159

the blame for the stale and meaningless geometry that has proliferated in architecture all over the world, as well as share the credit for the general improvement in product and graphic design. However, the De Stijl conception emerges, in retrospect, as the more imaginative. As the English architect, Brian Housden, has written:

Bauhaus designers were very successful in getting tubular furniture, ceramics, electrical fittings, and kitchen equipment into production, and their designs were good by any standard. Unlike De Stijl work, however, these designs were conceived within an existing tradition, whose main characteristics were reductive. Members of De Stijl, after reducing their designs, then used their imaginations to create a new and exciting world; Bauhaus designers left their work arid and impersonal. It is the imaginative content of many of the products of De Stijl which makes our interest in them more lasting. (*Design*, March 1968)

If De Stijl is partly responsible for the worst anonymities of the international style in architecture this is mainly because of the blind following today of the principles of forty or fifty years ago. Throughout the fourteen years of De Stijl's existence van Doesburg was prepared to modify and change his ideas according to the changing circumstances of the times which demanded new thinking. Were he alive today he would no doubt, as would Lissitzky or Moholy-Nagy, be working in a totally different way from the 'twenties and 'thirties, in a style suited to the needs of our own age.

The statements issued in *De Stijl* were often dogmatic and aggressive. But the objects, buildings and paintings produced by those associated with De Stijl speak otherwise. Mondrian loved the city and hated the greenery of the countryside in his later years, yet his paintings have a spiritual and mystical depth, an invitation to meditation that is closer to eastern religious belief than to a naïve and optimistic faith in western technology. Van Doesburg's decorations for the Café Aubette (with those of Arp and Sophie Taüber-Arp) must have created an exhilarating and stimulating environment that wonderfully conveyed the sense of being alive in the twentieth century without becoming crudely mechanistic or inhuman. Oud pioneered low-cost, standardized housing

Theo van Doesburg and **Cornelis van Eesteren** Design for a shopping
arcade and café (not executed)
From *De Stijl* 1925

and yet his Café Unie and the little temporary manager's hut
were personal works of great subtlety and grace. Rietveld's
Schröder house and furniture are statements about the nature of
space. Not a vague, abstract idea of space, but space as the relationship between human beings and the environment in which
we live.

Rietveld's zig-zag chair (1934) was his only wooden chair to have been produced and sold in quantity. (It was made in series of twenty during the 'thirties.) Like the red-blue chair it embodies the act of sitting as being active, not passive. But it is more dynamic than the red-blue chair, closer to van Doesburg's counter-compositions. The Z-chair is crouched like a cat, relaxed and yet tense with the possibility of quick and decisive movement.

Rietveld wanted to make the chair in one piece, but the techniques to do this were not available at the time. There are now appearing one-piece chairs based on Rietveld's Z-chair. This book began with Rietveld's red-blue chair as embodying the most important principles of De Stijl. It can appropriately end with his zig-zag chair which links De Stijl with our own time.

Gerrit Rietveld Zig-zag chair, 1934

Acknowledgements and Short Bibliography

I would like to thank the following people for their help : Bernard Gay (who organized the De Stijl exhibition at the Camden Arts Centre, London, in 1968) ; Brian Housden (whose fine collection of Rietveld furniture is illustrated in colour on page 58) ; Mrs T. Schröder-Schräder of the Schröder house, Utrecht ; Mrs J.M.A. Oud-Dinaux, the widow of J.J.P.Oud ; and J.Leering, Director of the Stedelijk van Abbemuseum, Eindhoven.

Anyone who writes on De Stijl will have to depend to a large extent on H.L.C.Jaffés *De Stijl 1917–1932* (Tiranti, London), and I would like to acknowledge my debt to this and to thank Professor Jaffé for generously allowing me to quote from some of his translations from the Dutch.

Jaffé's book is less concerned with De Stijl architecture than with De Stijl painting (and with that of Mondrian in particular). A good account of the development of De Stijl architecture and its relationship to international developments is to be found in Reyner Banham's *Theory and Design in the First Machine Age* (Architectural Press, London). Theodore Brown's *Gerrit Rietveld: Architect* (Bruna & Zoon, Utrecht) is a model of what an architectural monograph should be and I should like to thank the publishers for permission to quote from Brown's translations of Rietveld's writings and for kindly allowing the reproduction here of several illustrations.

The *De Stijl* magazine has recently been reprinted in its entirety by Athenaeum, Amsterdam, Bert Bakker, The Hague and Polak and Van Gennep, Amsterdam, who have kindly granted me permission to reproduce several illustrations from *De Stijl*. A final volume of translations of the Dutch text into English is to follow.

Form magazine (85, Norwich Street, Cambridge) published translations of articles on architecture from the *De Stijl* magazine in *Form 5* (September 1967) ; and in *Form 6* (December 1967) and in *Form 7* (March 1968) a complete index to the *De Stijl* magazine. Van Doesburg's Bauhaus Book has been published in translation as *Principles of Neo-Plastic Art* (Lund Humphries, London).

Vantongerloo's *Paintings, Sculptures, Reflections* and Mondrian's *Plastic Art and Pure Plastic Art and other Essays* are published by George Wittenborn, New York. The standard work on Mondrian is Michel Seuphor's *Piet Mondrian* (Thames and Hudson, London), which contains a classified catalogue of Mondrian's work. Alfred H.Barr's useful pamphlet *De Stijl* is published by the Museum of Modern Art. A comprehensive bibliography is to be found in Jaffé.

Index

STUDIO VISTA/DUTTON PICTUREBACKS

edited by David Herbert

British churches by Edwin Smith and Olive Cook
Great modern architecture by Sherban Cantacuzino
European domestic architecture by Sherban Cantacuzino
Modern churches of the world
by Robert Maguire and Keith Murray
Modern houses of the world by Sherban Cantacuzino

African sculpture by William Fagg and Margaret Plass
Florentine sculpture by Anthony Bertram
Greek sculpture by John Barron
Indian sculpture by Philip Rawson
Modern sculpture by Alan Bowness
Michelangelo by Anthony Bertram

Art deco by Bevis Hillier
Art nouveau by Mario Amaya
De Stijl by Paul Overy
Pop art: object and image by Christopher Finch
The Bauhaus by Gillian Naylor
1000 years of drawing by Anthony Bertram
Modern graphics by Keith Murgatroyd

Arms and armour by Howard L. Blackmore
The art of the garden by Miles Hadfield
Art in silver and gold by Gerald Taylor
Firearms by Howard L. Blackmore
Jewelry by Graham Hughes
Costume in pictures by Phillis Cunnington
Modern furniture by Ella Moody
Modern ceramics by Geoffrey Beard
Modern glass by Geoffrey Beard
Motoring history by L. T. C. Rolt
Railway history by C. Hamilton Ellis
Toys by Patrick Murray

Charlie Chaplin: early comedies by Isabel Quigly
The films of Alfred Hitchcock by George Perry
Greta Garbo by Raymond Durgnat and John Kobal
Marlene Dietrich by John Kobal
Movie monsters by Denis Gifford
New cinema in Britain by Roger Manvell
New cinema in Europe by Roger Manvell
New cinema in the USA by Roger Manvell
The great funnies by David Robinson
The silent cinema by Liam O'Leary